SKILLS, KNOWLEDGE, AND PRACTICAL STRATEGIES FOR EVERYDAY LIFE

# Young Adult Road Map

## A Step-By-Step Guide to Navigating Wellness, Independent Living, and Transition Services for People in Their Teens and Twenties

**By Wendy Lowe Besmann and Kimberly Douglass, PhD**

**With the Young Adult Road Map Editorial Board:**
Joshua Calarino, Lead; Justine Castaneda, Heather Hall, Shelby Haisley, Olivia Kane, Zachary Karenchak, Jasmine Marshall, Adam Nooe, Alyse Schwartz, and Sebastian Serrano-Johnson

Illustrations by Danyell Thillet
Edited by Heather Hall, MS

D1597776

GET THERE PROJECT
NATIONAL LEARNING COLLABORATIVE

MELTON HILL MEDIA
Find a path... and leave a trail.

From the publisher
of **Family Road Map**

For use of this book, Get There Project, a training academy and learning portal, has developed training curricula geared towards social workers, counselors, clinicians, family support partners, parents, case managers, and school staff. **For more information, visit https:// getthereproject.org.** In 2018, Team Up for Families (TUFF), was chartered as a non-profit, family-run organization for the purpose of partnering with other agencies to study the effectiveness of navigation training curricula in supporting and increasing access to appropriate services for children, youth, and young adults with special needs. **For more information, please contact info@teamupforfamilies.org.**

Printed in the United States of America. This book is printed on acid-free paper.
Last digit is print number: 9 8 7 6 5 4 3 2 1

Published by Melton Hill Media, LLC. 9119 Solway Ferry Road, Oak Ridge, TN 37830
www.meltonhillmedia.com

Library of Congress Cataloging-in-Publication Data: Besmann, Wendy Lowe and Douglass, Kimberly

Young Adult Road Map: A Step-By-Step Guide to Navigating Wellness, Independent Living, and Transition Services for People in Their Teens and Twenties.

Includes bibliographical references ISBN-13 978-0-9816793-6-5

1.      Young Adult Non-Fiction (Special Needs)
2.      Young Adult Non-Fiction (Intellectual and Developmental)
3.      Young Adult Non-Fiction (Health--Behavioral and Emotional)

Library of Congress Control Number: 2018936316

# Table of Contents

## About Get There Project and Team Up for Families (TUFF)

Team Up for Families was created in 2007 as a peer-based initiative to develop and distribute materials that would help special needs families navigate service systems. By the end of 2018, "Road Map" workshops and coaching curricula had served more than 600 family members in eight states. That same year, TUFF was incorporated as a family-run non-profit organization. "Get There Project" is an ongoing partnership between TUFF and Melton Hill Media, LLC, publisher of **Family Road Map** and **Young Adult Road Map**. Get There Project produces and evaluates new media designed to help people manage complicated problems through step-by-step strategic thinking. For more details, please contact **info@gettthereproject.org.**

## About the Authors

Wendy Besmann, the mother of a son with autism and bipolar disorder, is Director of Get There Project, President of Melton Hill Media, and founder of TUFF. While working with a federally-funded system of care for transition-age youth in Knox County, Tennessee, she trained staff to use High Fidelity Wraparound, a strengths-based approach to serving the complex needs of children, youth, and their families. She is the author of **Team Up for Your Child: A Step-By-Step Guide to Working Smarter with Doctors, Schools, Insurers, and Agencies** (2008, 2012), **Family Road Map: A Step-By-Step Guide to Navigating Health, Education, and Insurance Systems for Families with Special Needs** (2017), and co-author of **Family Road Map Lesson Plan** (2017). Her work has appeared in numerous publications, including the journal *Emotional and Behavioral Support in Youth*.

Kimberly Douglass, PhD, has many years of experience seeking services for family members and friends with special needs. Douglass is an Associate Dean and Associate Professor at Memphis State University. She is an award-winning instructor who addresses the social justice concerns of youth and young adults with special needs in her teaching and research. Her current research examines quality of life among transition age youth. Douglass has led projects funded by the National Science Foundation and the Institute for Museum and Library Services.

## About the Illustrator

Danyell Thillet is an artist, illustrator, and writer, living in Brooklyn with her spouse and an orange cat. She is a graduate of Purchase College, State University of New York, as part of their prestigious Art+Design program. Her work has been exhibited in the New York Metropolitan area, as well as in national galleries and has been featured in independent magazines. Her solo exhibition, Feels Like Home (2010) showed at Fringe Salon in Manhattan. Much of that collection can still be seen at danyellthillet.com. Her (mostly) autobiographic webcomic, *Sorry, I Was Just Talking to Myself,* publishes weekly on Tumblr.

## About the Editor

Heather Hall, MS, is Executive Director of Team Up for Families. She also served as the editor of **Family Road Map**. She is the lead author of the **Family Road Map** Lesson Plan and **Young Adult Road Map** Lesson Plan curricula. She also serves as a member of the Young Adult Road Map Editorial Board.

**Young Adult Road Map Editorial Board Members**: Joshua Calarino, Lead; Justine Castaneda, Heather Hall, Shelby Haisley, Olivia Kane, Zachary Karenchak, Jasmine Marshall, Adam Nooe, Alyse Schwartz, and Sebastian Serrano-Johnson. (Please see page 8 for more about the Young Adult Road Map Editorial Board.)

Design and production by Barbara Boeing, Boeing Design and Illustration

## The Road to Finding Out Where YOU Fit In

Sooner or later, almost every teen or young adult is asked **THE QUESTION**. It comes out something like, "What are your plans?" or "What do you want to do?" or "What do want to BE?" **THE QUESTION** can seem totally stressful when you are dealing with other big challenges. Maybe you need to spend a lot of energy getting well or staying well. Maybe you live with a disability or a developmental issue. Maybe a state agency has been involved with determining where you go and what you do. It can feel as if people expect you to cruise through your 20s with everything all figured out.

## To De-Stress the Situation, Change the Conversation

If **THE QUESTION** feels wrong to you right now, consider changing the conversation. Ask yourself: "**How do I picture the everyday life I want to live as an independent adult?**" That picture may have several "focus areas." It will probably include a place to live in a certain city or neighborhood, good relationships, activities you enjoy, school or a job, and enough money to meet your needs. Where do you want to wake up in the morning? What do you want to do all day? What kind of people do you want to hang out with at work or in your free time?

When you think about the various parts of an everyday life that could make you feel safe and happy, the picture of your future starts coming into view. The whole picture doesn't usually come together right away. Most people need to try different experiences and learn more about their options to find out where they fit in. However, imagining what a good day might look like in the next few years of your life can make it easier to set practical goals. You don't need to figure it all out right now. Starting from where you stand at this moment, you can take it one step at a time.

*At age 18 in our society, everything changes. You have more responsibilities, but you also have more choices. You have the power to make your own decisions and speak for yourself, in your own voice.*

## Your Transition Job Description

The period between age 14 and 26 (sometimes up to age 30) is often called "**Transition to Adulthood**" or "**Emerging Adulthood**" because becoming an adult is a process. No one wakes up one day as an adult. You grow into adulthood at your own pace. In a perfect (and perfectly boring) TV movie, everybody gets a driver's license, goes to prom, ships off to college, and scores a great job on schedule. However, the reality is we all have our own transition timelines. That's OK. It's YOUR life.

In childhood, other people had legal responsibility for making decisions that affected you. Your choices were limited. Other people spoke for you. At age 18 in our society, everything changes. You have more responsibilities, but you also have more choices. You have the power to make your own decisions and speak for yourself, in your own voice. Your #1 Transition Job Description is to learn and do what you need to live the life you want— right now, a few years down the road, and in the more distant future. That means asking questions and learning strategies for getting the help you need.

CHOICES

ROAD TO THE FUTURE

RESPONSIBILITIES

## Step-By-Step Strategies for Navigating Systems

To build the life you want, you need support to reach goals and solve problems. That support usually comes from **services provided by organized systems**. Some people talk about "The System" as something that is unfair or doesn't meet their needs (which may be true in some cases). However, the term system used in this Guide refers to any one of the organizations and agencies that provide a service to youth or young adults. This could be a mental health center, a hospital, a walk-in clinic in a neighborhood drug store, or a housing benefits office. It could be an insurance company you call on the phone. It could be the court system or a rehab program. It could be a college or training school.

Finding services in this world is called navigating systems. Like countries, each of these systems has its own language, rules, and procedures. If you have already received services for a while, somebody navigated systems for you. To live an independent life, you must navigate certain systems by yourself. However, finding your own way can feel very frustrating. That's why you need a road map. It lets you focus on taking one step at a time, and gives you strategies for getting where you need to go. *Young Adult Road Map* is a step-by-step Guide to navigating systems, whether you are an older teen approaching legal adulthood or someone moving through your twenties.

## The Guiding Star for Navigating Systems

As you move through systems looking for services, the journey can be confusing. The *Guiding Star* can help you stay on the right road. The five points of the *Guiding Star* are five tasks that will keep you on the path to help no matter what system you enter. This Guide can help you sort through all the confusion and chunk up a big job into smaller jobs you can handle. This Guide is organized into simple, step-by-strategies that use all five points of the *Guiding Star*.

1. **SET GOALS.** Decide what to look for based on your strengths and concerns. What do you already have and what do you need right now to take the next steps? Life is simpler when everyone who can support you understands your priorities.

2. **LEARN SYSTEM BASICS.** Get to know key words, procedures, and provider roles so you understand what choices you have, where to find services, and how to get those services.

3. **BUILD RELATIONSHIPS.** Communicate your priorities clearly. Show you expect to be included in all decisions as a full partner. Find people who can help you meet goals and solve problems.

4. **MANAGE INFORMATION.** Keep good records. Track and report your progress so medical providers and others can understand how you are doing. Insist on clear explanations of any evaluations or reports that are used to make decisions about you.

5. **FIND SUPPORT.** Create a network of people and resources that can help you stay safe and cope with challenges along your journey.

## PARTS OF THE PICTURE

When you picture how you want to live as an independent adult, it helps to think about the "focus areas" of everyday living. These might include:

- **Employment:** Satisfying work (and whatever education/training it takes to get that work)

- **Housing:** A safe and comfortable place to live

- **Transportation:** Reliable, affordable ways to get around

- **Community:** Friends, loved ones, and people or organizations to support you when you need it

- **Health:** Good insurance, the right providers (doctors, dentists, therapists), a wellness plan, knowledge about how and where to get services in your area

- **Purpose:** Things that give your life meaning and fulfillment. For some people, this can include pursuing creative arts (such as poetry or dance), practicing a religious faith, working for a cause, or doing service for others.

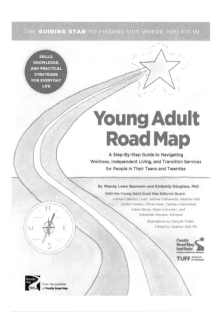

About **Young Adult Road Map**: This Guide is based, in part, on the related **Family Road Map** Guide and curriculum, which was created to help family caregivers of children and youth with special needs get services. Additional content was written by members of the Young Adult Road Map Editorial Board. Family Road Map Institute and Team Up for Families (TUFF) gratefully acknowledges the assistance and encouragement of the National Federation of Families for Children's Mental Health and Youth M.O.V.E. National, which helped to organize the first Young Adult Road Map content meeting at the NFFCMH 2016 Annual Conference in Phoenix, Arizona. Seven participants in that one-day session later joined the Young Adult Road Map Editorial Board, collaborating in the development of this Guide and curriculum.

# Symbols in this Guide

 Key words used in systems

 Resources in print

 Useful apps

 Online content

 Important alerts

 Good ideas

 Try this

 Resource in Spanish

 Paperwork solutions

 "Scripts" for talking to providers

THE BIG PICTURE

TRANSITION FOCUS

GUIDING STAR
POINT ONE:

# Set Goals

Decide what to look for based on your
strengths and concerns. What do you
already have, and what do you need
right now to take the next steps?

**YOU
ARE
HERE**

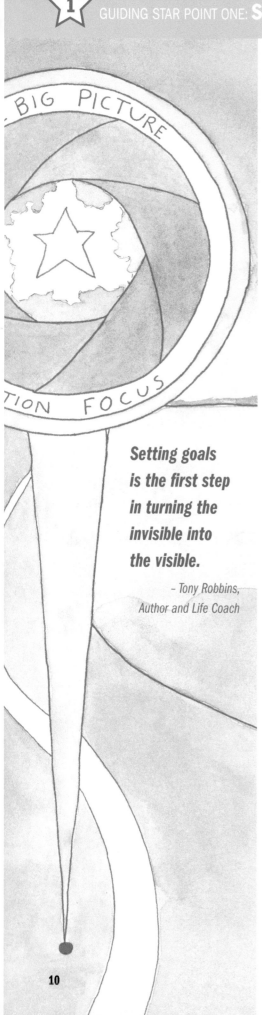

*Setting goals is the first step in turning the invisible into the visible.*

– Tony Robbins,
*Author and Life Coach*

## Why Set Goals?

How many times have you heard someone say, "You have your whole life ahead of you?" They are thinking about all the good things life can bring you in the future. Yet the future can seem frightening, too. Sometimes "The Future" looks like a big, hazy cloud in the distance. All you can see close-up are problems along the road. These problems may have scary labels such as "not enough money" or "where will I live?" The *Guiding Star* can help you move ahead by sorting out problems into manageable chunks. It starts with using your own voice to *change the conversation* about your future.

Guiding Star Point One—SET GOALS--is a conversation about turning PROBLEMS into PRIORITIES. This is a person-centered conversation, because it is about what you need. You must lead this conversation because you are the only person who really knows what you think, what you feel, and what concerns you. ***You are the expert about yourself.***

## Part One: **FIVE KINDS OF STRENGTHS**

The conversation begins with your strengths. However, this isn't just a "feel-good" exercise. Your strengths, plus the services and supports you will find on your journey, can solve many problems along the road to the life you want.

**YOUR STRENGTHS + SERVICES AND SUPPORTS = SOLUTIONS TO PROBLEMS**

Examining your strengths is like packing for a journey. Before you set out, it's a good idea to check your pockets/purse/backpack or the trunk of your car for any items that might come in handy down the road. You don't need to figure out exactly how they might be useful right now. You just need to be aware of your strengths, and let others who support you know about them, too. Amazing things can happen when your strengths are carefully examined.

🌟 **See Activity 1.1, What Are My Strengths?**

To start, think about five different kinds of strengths:

**1.** **Qualities**—Personal traits such as persistence and loyalty to friends, as well as the habit of speaking respectfully to others, a willingness to take directions from a supervisor, or the capacity to stay calm in a crisis.

**2.** **Abilities**—What a person can do. These might include a learned skill, such as baking great cookies or playing an instrument. They could also include a talent, like being a great organizer or learning quickly by observing others.

**3.** **Interests**—What you like to do, what motivates you or makes you curious, or a hobby you like to do in your spare time.

**4.** **Assets**—Things you own or can use, such as a car, a monthly bus pass, insurance, or safe housing.

**5.** **Resources**—People and organizations that can help if you need it. These might include a drop-in center, church that provides food assistance, a neighbor who can give you a place to stay in an emergency, a job training program, or a local library that provides computers with free internet.

## Part Two: WHAT ARE YOUR CONCERNS?

The next step in this conversation is to think about your concerns. These are problems you are dealing with now or things you worry about for the future. Below are some common types of concerns for young adults. If you have a concern under one of these columns, decide whether to list it under the row marked "Right now," "One year from now," or "Two to three years from now." (Just make your best guess.) Jot down a few details about each concern.

❋ **See Activity 1.2, What are My Concerns?**

**Physical health** (physical sensations in your body)

**Emotional health** (thoughts, feelings, and behavior toward others)

**Relationships** (for example, with friends/family/others around you)

**Housing** (whether you have a stable place to live)

**Transportation** (affordable, safe ways to get around)

**Education** (or training for employment)

**Income** (enough money to meet daily living expenses)

## Part Three: SETTING PRIORITIES

Look at the concerns you listed for "Right now." Circle the top three concerns for which you would like help or support. These might include concerns that interfere with your life or well-being (such as an emotional health challenge). A priority concern could also be an opportunity in your life (such as an approaching deadline for college financial aid).

Using these worksheets, you can invite mentors into your life (such as counselors, family members, or peer coaches) to enter this conversation. You can ask for advice about which systems will help you with your concerns and what specific actions you might take right now. Your mentors may suggest additional goals or a shift in priorities. That's OK. However, the point of this step is to **plan at least one action you can take** toward working on your priority concerns. If the people around you can't suggest an action that seems right, don't give up. You may need to learn more about a system (for example, housing) to find the right mentors or providers to advise you. Read more about that in Guiding Star Point Two, "Learn System Basics."

## Part Four: "THE BIG PICTURE"

The final step in setting goals is to look at "The Big Picture" of what you want your everyday life to look like (either soon or someday) as an independent adult. Seeing "The Big Picture" is like watching scenes from a movie with a happy ending and noticing all the little details. When you picture how you want to live as an independent adult, it helps to think about the "focus areas" of everyday living.

## LIFE SKILLS COACHES

A Life Skills Development Coach can help with all services related to living, learning, working, structuring, and planning time. They work with patients to fulfill their dreams in all life areas, despite any obstacles they may have. For example, a Life Skills Development Coach may do weekly or daily check-ins with the patient to ensure they are staying on track.

*(Source: LindnerCenterofHope.org)*

EDITORIAL BOARD NOTES
Contributed by: Alyse Schwartz

*"A lot of times we base everything just on our immediate circumstance. We don't see a big picture for our lives."*

*– Jennifer Holliday, singer and actor*

## BEFORE AND AFTER PANIC ATTACKS

BEFORE:

What was I thinking about?

How did I react to my thoughts?

Where was I?

What was I eating?

Who was I with?

AFTER:

What else can I think about?

How is my breath?

How long did it take me to return to normal?

## INTROSPECTION:

Looking at yourself and recognizing the things that may trigger you, what happens when you are triggered, and what happens after you are triggered can be very helpful. These steps allow you to understand what to avoid and what to do once the trigger has occurred. One very good resource is the Wellness Recovery Action Plan (WRAP). Being able to recognize when you may be in crisis and having a plan set to deal with it can work wonders for your mental health and overall well-being. The ability to look internally and place yourself in the "then," "now," and "tomorrow" allows you to be grounded and learn how to make progress to a better you.

These "focus areas" might include:

- **Housing:** A safe and comfortable place to live
- **Employment:** Satisfying work (and whatever education/training it takes to get that work)
- **Transportation:** Reliable, affordable ways to get around
- **Community:** Friends, loved ones, and people or organizations to help you when you need it
- **Health:** Good insurance, the right providers (doctors, dentists, therapists), a wellness plan, and knowledge about how and where to get services in your area
- **Things that give your life meaning and fulfillment:** For some people this can include pursuing creative arts (such as poetry or dance), practicing a religious faith, working for a cause, or doing service for others.

Jot down a few words or phrases that describe any ideas that come to mind. You may not be able to imagine the whole picture. That's OK. However, starting to imagine your everyday life can help you set long term goals. It can also help you speak your truth to the people around you. That will be very important as you look for help in systems.

✳ **See Activity 1.3, The Big Picture**

## YOU ARE HERE:

## Guiding Star Point One Review

Your #1 Transition Job Description is to learn and do what it takes to live the life you want. If that future seems uncertain, you can *change the conversation* about your future. Doing that helps you move forward (from where you stand right now), one step at a time. One way to start this process is to:

1. Make a list of your strengths, because your strengths plus the services and supports you will find will lead to solutions to your concerns. Services and supports are things such as treatments, benefits, training, housing vouchers, counseling, etc., that may help you live the life you want.

2. Make a list of concerns that affect different parts of your life.

3. Begin thinking about "The Big Picture" of the everyday life you want to live.

4. Begin talking to others about those strengths and concerns to find out what services and supports you might need.

GUIDING STAR
POINT TWO:

# Learn System Basics

Become familiar with key words,
procedures, and provider roles so
you understand what choices
you have, where to find services,
and how to get those services.

**YOU ARE HERE**

## Why Learn About Systems?

Every day, you probably encounter many different systems. A system is just any group of people and things that are organized to operate together. Schools, religious communities (such as churches), health centers, youth organizations, and social agencies are all types of systems. Each system has its own language, its own way of doing things, and people who take on different jobs (sometimes called roles) as part of that system.

To *change the conversation* about your future, you will need to talk with people in one or more systems about your strengths and concerns. You will need to use your own voice to find the right help. However, for this part of the conversation, you will need to learn some of that system's key (important) words and typical ways of getting things done. It's kind of like going to a foreign country. To find your way around, you must learn to speak a bit of the language, understand the important rules of the place, meet some people, and find out how they can help you. Once you have that basic knowledge, you can feel a lot more confident looking for what you need.

> Change the conversation

## Key Words Open Doors

Your everyday life may be affected by many systems: medical, mental health, social welfare, education, transportation, housing, etc. Every system has key words that people use to exchange important information and decide whether someone is eligible to get services. Those key words really do open doors! However, different systems use the same words to mean different types of procedures, or ways of doing things. For example, the term evaluation (a conclusion—usually some kind of report—on a situation's causes and what needs to be done) can mean one thing in a medical center, but mean a very different procedure in a school system. That is one more reason why it's important to learn the system basics that affect you.

## Part One: MEDICAL AND BEHAVIORAL SYSTEMS

For young adults who may have issues with behavior or development, medical and behavioral assessments are important first steps to getting to services. *(What this means: If you have concerns about your thoughts, feelings, or actions toward yourself or others, you should talk to a provider about getting a medical and behavioral assessment.)* An assessment documents (provides information or proof in your records) that you have certain conditions or needs. For example, it may document that you need special support when you attend college or begin a training program after high school. It may document that you need transportation supports (help getting from place to place, such as a bus pass or transportation voucher) or mobility supports (help getting around, such as a wheelchair or walker). It may document that you need special services to find and maintain a job. Even if you have been diagnosed before, or have had a diagnosis for a long time, you may need to be tested again. It's important to be open to re-testing, because your body and brain change as you grow. Also, you may need re-testing to qualify for benefits in some adult systems, such as Social Security.

## Key Words for First Steps

In health systems, a **diagnosis** is the overall word that health providers use to describe a problem. It is reached through an **assessment** (some way of studying the person) by gathering enough **evidence** (facts) for a report about what needs to be done, usually called an **evaluation**. Evidence may come from conversations with you or somebody else about **symptoms**, which are changes or problems with physical, mental, or emotional conditions. Other facts may come from **physical examinations**, tests, or laboratory studies. The evaluation and diagnosis may be used to make a **treatment plan** (steps you will take to work on the problem) or to inform others who will get involved. These facts may also be used to decide whether you can get certain health expenses paid for by your insurance plan. They may help determine whether you can receive special services, such as **special education** or **vocational rehabilitation**.

## You Aren't a Label

A diagnosis is a guideline, not a recipe! Your body, brain, and emotions are different from another person's body, brain, and emotions. Those differences will affect the kinds of medications or therapies that work best for you. You may meet some of the **criteria** (types of symptoms) for two different disorders. One may be called a **primary disorder** (main disorder) while the other one may be called a **secondary disorder** or **comorbid diagnosis**. The diagnosis may change as you grow older or as more information is gathered. (Different providers may also disagree about what your symptoms mean and what should be done to treat those symptoms. That's one big reason why you must learn to navigate systems and make your own healthcare decisions!)

Do you worry about being labeled with a diagnosis? If you received services as a child, you may be used to labels that describe your conditions or behaviors. However, labels cannot tell you everything there is to know about yourself. A diagnosis offers you and others in your life a way to think about what is happening with you. While a diagnosis does not tell the whole story, it should help you get the services you need. It can help others understand you better.

**Look Up Those L-o-o-n-g, Confusing Words**

To find definitions of all key words printed like **this**, go to the Glossary section of *Young Adult Road Map*, which begins on page 71.

## WHAT'S A "PROVIDER?"

The organizations that give health and social services are often called providers. Some **providers** have private practices that employ only one or a few staff members. Some private behavioral health practices are attached to hospitals or clinics. A larger organization that provides behavioral health services may be called a **CMHC (Community Mental Health Center)**, a **CMHO (Community Mental Health Organization)**, or **CMHA (Community Mental Health Agency)**. These organizations may employ many psychiatrists, psychologists, social workers, case managers, and support staff.

# Five Rules for the Road

## KNOW YOUR SUPPORT STAFF

Receptionists, physicians' assistants, administrators, technicians, and nurses can be great sources of information about how things work in a provider's offce or clinic. Take time to notice them, learn their names, and ask for their advice.

**1.** **Think Primary First:** Understanding yourself starts with a physical examination by a primary care provider. This person is sometimes known as a "primary care practitioner," or "family medicine practitioner." In some cases, you will see a Nurse Practitioner (NP). Even if the doctor has already done a regular physical exam, he or she may order special tests or ask different questions. Some behavioral problems can be caused by physical conditions; for example, certain brain injuries or fevers may affect behavior. Also, some health problems may lead to behavioral or emotional issues. If that's the case, your doctor may want to refer you to a medical specialist or a behavioral health specialist.

**2.** **Take Your Records:** Be sure to bring any physical examination records to any specialists who evaluate or treat you, since they may not do full examinations themselves. This information is also important when you fill out health history forms, which you may need to do each time you visit a new provider.

**3.** **Ask what, why and "Can you explain?" questions:** If a med is being prescribed, make sure you understand and agree with the provider's decision. In some rural counties and other areas that are short on behavioral health providers, the primary care doctor may prescribe medications for behavioral health issues. (Some primary care doctors have special training for this.) In some cases, a doctor may order a blood test or other procedure to find out if a medical condition is causing your atypical behavior. **It is important to know that no current medical test can diagnose conditions such as ADHD or anxiety. The provider must rely on observation and information provided by you.**

**4.** **Keep primary care providers in the loop:** If your treatment begins with a psychiatrist or other behavioral health specialist, be sure to keep the primary care provider informed and involved. For example, certain medications for ADHD or mood disorders can affect your weight or risk for diseases, such as diabetes. If so, your primary care doctor can work with you on a plan to prevent or treat such conditions before they become big problems for you.

**5.** **Ask before trying alternatives:** Many people are interested in "alternative" medicine therapies (which might include herbal treatments, massage, meditation, or acupuncture). Some alternatives can be very useful. If you think one of these might be right for you, be sure to check with your primary care provider first. You need to make sure they are not harmful and will not interfere with an existing condition or medication you are taking.

# Who's Who in Health Care

Medical, behavioral, and developmental health specialists who may **evaluate** you include:

**MEDICAL DOCTORS AND NURSES <u>who can prescribe medications</u>:**

*Primary Care Physician:* A medical doctor who handles routine checkups and general medical needs. Note: Some people go to a Licensed Nurse Practitioner (see below) for this purpose.

*Psychiatrist:* A medical doctor who is trained to evaluate and treat you, primarily by prescribing medications. A psychiatrist has the most formal training in behavioral health, but may spend the least amount of time with you during treatment.

*Behavioral/Developmental Pediatrician:* Combines physical, psychological, and developmental evaluations, as well as treatment.

*Neurologist:* Medical doctor who specializes in how the brain functions physically and chemically.

*Licensed Nurse Practitioner:* Assists in or performs clinical evaluations, designs treatment plans, and may provide counseling, medication management, and/or other treatment. May work in a primary care practice. A Psychiatric-Mental Health Nurse Practitioner (PMHNP) does mental health management.

*Physician's Assistant:* A person certified to provide basic medical services. A Physician's Assistant may take medical histories, do physical exams, take blood and urine samples, care for wounds, and give injections and immunizations. When you go to walk-in clinic, you will usually see a Licensed Nurse Practitioner or a Physician's Assistant.

**BEHAVIORAL (MENTAL) HEALTH PROVIDERS <u>who may evaluate or treat, but do NOT prescribe medications</u>:**

*Clinical Psychologist:* Licensed by the state to evaluate your behavioral health. May also provide **psychotherapy**, a form of counseling that is commonly known as "talk therapy," but may include other kinds of one-on-one or group treatment.

*Licensed Clinical Social Worker:* Licensed by the state to provide one-on-one or group therapy.

*Counseling and Evaluation Providers:* Some providers (including those listed above) may have other titles, such as Licensed Psychological Examiner, Licensed Marriage and Family Therapist, Licensed Professional Counselor, or Licensed Substance Abuse Counselor. Feel free to ask questions about the therapist's training. His or her license should be posted somewhere in the building.

## FAQs

The National Institute for Mental Health offers a useful booklet on behavioral health. Go to http://nimh.nih.gov/health/publications/index.shtml. It describes the treatments and medications most often used, and it answers frequently asked questions. You can order free booklets in English or Spanish.

¡En Español!

## STRAIGHT TALK

Sometimes it can be very hard to speak frankly about your problems. You may wonder if you are "making too much of it." It may not be part of your culture to tell personal information to people outside the family. In any case, it is very important to state the facts as clearly and plainly as you can from your own point of view. Tell the provider exactly what you observed, what you think, and what you feel. ***You are the expert about yourself.*** See "Getting Ready for Intake Interviews" for more ideas.

# How to Prepare for Your First Appointment with a New Provider

It can be a little intimidating going to see a health provider for the first time. Here are some tips.

**1.** Bring your insurance card and a form of ID (driver's license, state ID, etc.) If you don't have insurance, your provider can help connect you to resources.

**2.** Start thinking about what you want to work on with your provider. What is your main concern currently? (Sometimes it helps to think of your TOP THREE concerns and label them first, second, and third. WRITE THEM DOWN. That will help you talk to the health provider in an organized way, and you will get more respect).

**3.** If you have any copies of your records, bring those with you as well. Your provider may have you sign a **release of information** (a document that, once signed, allows permission to forward your heath care information to other providers).

## Getting Ready for Intake Interviews

An **intake interview** is the first appointment with a new health provider or agency. At this appointment, you will be asked to tell the provider about you and your symptoms.

**Symptoms** are signs of **disorders** (physical changes, thoughts, feelings, or behaviors that cause problems with functioning in everyday life).

## Choosing Someone to Evaluate You

A primary care provider may give you a referral (a medical order allowing you to see another provider) for a specific clinic, doctor, or other specialist(s). You may be concerned about a problem and decide to look for help on your own. You may have to pick someone from the list of providers in your insurance network. Sometimes it is necessary to switch from a pediatric (children's) provider or service system to an adult provider or system. If you are over 18, you have the right to pick your own providers (even if you already go to a certain doctor or other provider). If you are satisfied, that's great. If not, ultimately the choice is up to YOU.

How do you pick the right provider? There are no simple answers. With some types of insurance, you may not need a referral. Call the number on your insurance card if you have questions about this.

Many young adults are bothered by the thought of going to someone who will ask them lots of personal questions. It's easy to understand that feeling. This person will ask a lot of questions about your family life. Your behavior will be observed. The evaluator will form an opinion of your situation from the way you talk, fill out forms, and answer questions.

## Talking to Therapists

"Clinician" or "Clinical provider" means someone who evaluates you and may later provide therapy.

The term "therapist" usually refers to a psychologist (PhD or PsyD), social worker (LCSW), or licensed counselor who provides "talk therapy."

If you are considering a behavioral health (mental health) clinician who has a private practice, try to talk to this person on the phone first. Ask questions like these:

1. How long have you been in practice?

2. How much of your practice is with young adults?

3. What type of degrees do you have?

4. I am having problems with... (explain problem very briefly). How commonly do you see young adults with this type of problem?

5. Can you please explain what the steps of the evaluation will be?

6. What sorts of tests do you generally use?

7. What do you charge?

8. Do you file insurance paperwork? What is your procedure for payment?

9. Can I contact you between appointments, if necessary?

10. How do you prefer to be contacted between visits?

### LOOK FOR CLUES, TRUST YOUR INSTINCTS

Remember, you also have the right to observe and evaluate the provider who will work with you. You are hiring that person to do a service for you. You are seeking help because you need to solve a problem. You can do that best when you feel comfortable giving someone all the necessary information. That means, you need someone who knows how to listen. The best clinician will gather the facts and not jump to conclusions. Even the most well-known or recommended person in town may not be the right match for you and your needs. You must trust your gut instinct. You must notice things, such as body language or the way the provider addresses you, that may hint about whether you and the provider will get along. Some people like to bring a relative or trusted friend along to the first appointment to get an another view and take notes on what was said.

## CODE WORDS

Clinical evaluation reports often include certain terms that are "code words" for things one provider tells another. They might contain sentences such as, "Jane was neatly groomed and appropriately dressed for the season." This means Jane can care for herself. Tip: If, despite your best efforts, you show up at the evaluation very messy, in shoes full of holes or wearing shorts on a freezing day, explain why to the evaluator. ("I know it looks strange, but wearing long pants makes me feel too confined.") If the hot water failed that morning and you couldn't take a shower, explain this. Don't be embarrassed, just frank. Remember, the clinician isn't a mind reader; he or she knows the situation is difficult for you. Full information can only help.

## Tips for a First Clinician Visit

1. **Pick up on the clues.** When you see a clinical provider for the first time, pay attention to small cues that could mean a lot. A good clinician will usually begin by asking something such as, "Why are you here?" He or she will clearly explain methods for working together, payment arrangements, and what your role in treatment will be. For example, the clinician might say, "After I meet with you for about three weeks, I'll want us to get together and review the treatment plan."

2. **What's your comfort level?** Pay attention to the person's manner and the office environment. Does the clinician make you feel comfortable? Do you feel your concerns are being heard? If the person is sending text messages or reading from a file rather than making direct eye contact while you are speaking, that is not respectful of you as a partner. (Remember, you should not be texting or looking at your phone, either.)

3. **Remember, you have a choice.** If you receive services from a large agency, one person may conduct the evaluation, and a different person may give therapy. Others, such as a nurse or psychiatrist, may oversee medication management. If one of these persons doesn't seem right to you, you can request someone else. Talk to your case manager if you don't know how to do this. If necessary, ask an administrator within the clinic.

Unfortunately, in some small cities and rural areas there aren't many clinicians, therapists, or psychiatrists. If you really don't think any of the providers seems right for you, find out whether it's practical to go to a larger city.

Of course, you may need to see the person for more than one visit before you make any final judgment. People don't always "click" right away.

## Understanding the Treatment Plan

Once the evaluation process is complete, the clinician will meet with you to develop a treatment plan. This can take several different forms. In some cases, there will be a written report, sometimes called a "**Clinical Evaluation Report**" or "**Clinical Assessment Report**." This report will state the reason(s) you were referred, sum up your health history, explain test results, and make recommendations for treatment.

Always be sure the evaluator gives you a dated copy of any report or treatment plan that concerns you. Often the clinician will go over a "draft" report so you can find any errors. *READ THE REPORT CAREFULLY.* Ask about any results or terms you don't understand. Pay attention to anything in the report about your past medications, illnesses, or your family history. Mark your corrections clearly on your copy and file it in your binder. Ask when you can expect to receive a final copy of the report. When you receive it, make sure the corrections were made. Save this copy. If you don't receive it when promised, ask again and keep asking. *It's very important to have an accurate evaluation report because it becomes part of your record.* Other providers who treat you may use parts of it in their own reports. The real facts can get lost.

# Treatment Plan Forms

Large clinics, hospitals, and CMHAs often use a standard form for the treatment plan. Most plans contain this type of information:

**STATEMENT OF THE PROBLEM:** This part should describe the problem or problems in plain words. It may also include the diagnosis. *Example:* "John is often physically aggressive with romantic partners. At home, John has been observed cycling rapidly between extreme irritation and sadness. Symptoms get worse in winter. Diagnosis: Bipolar disorder with rapid cycling and Seasonal Affective Disorder".

**LONG-TERM GOALS:** This is how the team pictures a good outcome of treatment. *Example:* "John will learn and practice successful methods for managing anger without aggression. John's moods will be stable enough throughout the year to allow him to function at home."

**SHORT-TERM GOALS:** These are specific goals the team will work on immediately. If possible, there should be some way to measure whether progress toward the goals is being made. These goals should include a date to review whether the plan is working. *Example:* "Episodes of physical aggression will be decreased by at least one outburst weekly. John will show increased mood stability over a period of one month. Review progress with patient after one month from start of treatment." (Remember: These are goals, not promises. It's hard to predict whether or how soon a person's behavior will change.)

**INTERVENTION PLAN:** This plan describes actions you will take to reach your goals. An intervention plan should always list what will be done, who will do it, and how often actions will happen. It should list a start date and an estimated date to complete or review the actions. The plan should also include what you and your supporters will do.

*Example:*

a. "Medications to be prescribed by Doctor A for aggression and mood stability. Weekly medication management by Nurse B until John is stable for one month. Review medication as needed.

b. Psychotherapy sessions with MSW Therapist C twice weekly.

c. Visit with life coach every two weeks."

**CRISIS PLAN:** If your condition poses a threat to you or others, this crisis plan should describe what steps will be taken if things get a lot worse. The plan should tell someone (asking for you) whom to contact first, such as the number of the local Mental Health Crisis or Specialized Crisis Service, which hospital will accept you in a crisis, and who will communicate with the hospital. Sometimes this plan is put on a separate form. Make sure it includes all necessary medications.

**OTHER INFORMATION AND NEEDS:** If you have special needs that affect the plan (such as a medical condition or disability), this should be stated on the treatment plan. If you don't agree with something on the plan, state what the problems are and discuss them with your providers. Ask about alternatives. Remember to put a copy of this treatment plan in your binder.

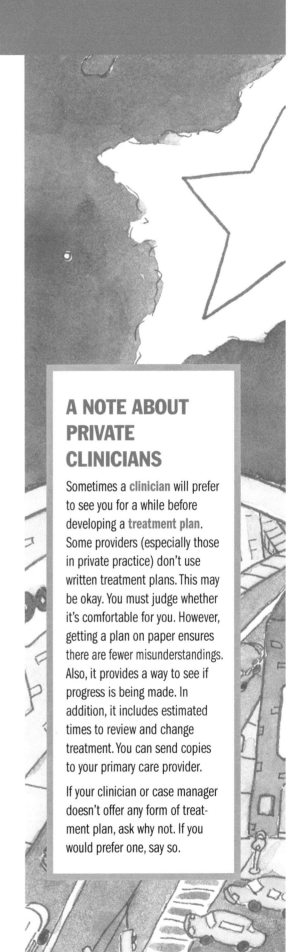

## A NOTE ABOUT PRIVATE CLINICIANS

Sometimes a clinician will prefer to see you for a while before developing a treatment plan. Some providers (especially those in private practice) don't use written treatment plans. This may be okay. You must judge whether it's comfortable for you. However, getting a plan on paper ensures there are fewer misunderstandings. Also, it provides a way to see if progress is being made. In addition, it includes estimated times to review and change treatment. You can send copies to your primary care provider.

If your clinician or case manager doesn't offer any form of treatment plan, ask why not. If you would prefer one, say so.

*In our American health care system, a lot depends on your insurance benefits.*

## Getting Medication Facts

If medication is part of your treatment plan, here are some questions you might ask the doctor or nurse:

1. How will this medication help me?

2. How commonly is the medication used by people my age?

3. Is this a brand-name medication? Is it available in a less expensive generic version?

4. What is the name of the generic version? Can I use it?

5. Can I switch between brands or between the generic and the brand-name medicine?

6. What is the dosage? Is it likely to change during the time I am getting used to it?

7. What if I can't swallow a pill or capsule? Is it available in chewable form or liquid? Can a pill be cut in half?

8. Will I need any laboratory tests with this medication? If so, how often?

## Part Two: HEALTH INSURANCE COVERAGE

Finding out **what** service you need is only part of the picture. Getting that service paid for is the other part. Most people find health insurance paperwork confusing at one point or another. It can look like an endless pile of forms covered with **number codes** and terms you don't understand. However, the information on those forms determines whether you get the treatment you need paid for by the insurance company.

In our American health care system, a lot depends on your insurance benefits. **Benefits** are payments made by the insurance company for services you receive. Sometimes this is called your **coverage**. Those benefits are part of a contract between you and the insurance company called an **insurance policy** or **insurance plan**. The rules of that plan may be complicated, and they may change over time. That's why there are MAPS and GUIDES.

**MAPS** are different forms of written information (such as a health plan **member's handbook**, an insurance plan website, or a government website) that explain benefits and procedures. These resources may tell you where to look for more information or what organizations can help you apply for benefits.

**GUIDES** are people who know about different parts of the process, such as customer service associates for insurance companies, case managers in Community Health Agencies, advocates, or staff in a medical office. **(For customer service, call the number on the back of your health insurance card, if you have one.)**

# Piecing Together the Insurance Puzzle

Why learn about insurance? If you know the system basics of health insurance, it will be much easier to understand maps and talk to guides. You can make better choices. You can avoid getting stuck with an insurance plan that costs too much or doesn't pay for or cover the services you need.

Every insurance plan is a kind of puzzle made up of four basic parts:

**1.** **Premium:** This is the amount you pay the insurance company to belong to the plan. In some plans, this premium is **subsidized** (paid for by a government agency). That part may change if your income changes—for example, once you get a full-time job.

**2.** **Coverage:** This piece of the puzzle looks at the types of services the plan will pay for, and who can provide you with those services (**in-network providers**). Your plan may still pay a smaller amount if you use providers who aren't on that list (called **out-of-network providers**).

**3.** **Out of Pocket:** This piece concerns two ways you may still have to use your own money to pay for some services. You may have a "**co-payment**" or "**co-pay**," which is an amount you pay every time you see a certain provider. You may also need to pay a certain amount of money for your health care treatment each year before the insurance company starts to pay. This is called a **deductible**. (Sometimes insurance plans with low premiums can have fairly high co-pays or deductibles.)

**4.** **Limits:** The last piece of the puzzle has to do with things your insurance plan will NOT cover. "**Caps**" are limits on the amounts of money the insurance plan will pay for certain services. **Exclusions** are types of services for which the plan will not pay. An **annual or lifetime maximum benefit** is the greatest amount the insurance company will pay for a certain type of service over one year (or the entire time you have that policy).

## LIFELINES

Below are two links to sample crisis plans:

https://magic.piktochart.com/output/3641390-how-to-create-a-safety-plan
(National Suicide Prevention Lifeline)

http://mentalhealthrecovery.com/wp-content/uploads/2015/07/CrisisPlan2012Manual.pdf (http://mentalhealthrecovery.com/contact-us/)

These are two apps (iTunes) for crisis/safety plans:

- ■ Suicide Safety Plan
- ■ Be Safe

**EDITORIAL BOARD NOTES**
Contributed by: Alyse Schwartz

---

**1.**

**The Premium Piece**

How much will I pay for this policy (plan)? How often will I pay this? What happens if my income changes?

**2.**

**The Coverage Piece**

What types of benefits does this plan cover and what providers can I use (network)?

**3.**

**The Out of Pocket Piece**

What will I pay at the time I get services (co-pay) or before the insurance starts paying (deductible)?

**4.**

**The Limits Piece**

When does my plan stop paying for certain services (caps)? What services are not covered (exclusions)?

## How Insurance Plans Compare

When there are so many types of insurance plans available, it's difficult to know which ones are best to meet your needs. Look at the table below to see the different types of plans, how you can be eligible for each, and the considerations to keep in mind.

| Source of Plan | Eligibility | Considerations |
|---|---|---|
| Parents'/caregivers' plan | Must be a dependent (claimed on parent/guardian's income tax form as relying on them for financial support). Must be less than 26 years old. | The stability of your relationship with your parents/caregivers is important, as they will need to handle the paperwork for you. |
| Public plan (such as Medicaid) | Must meet state requirements for income level or disability. | Income and eligibility requirements for people with disabilities are not the same for each state. Things change from one year to the next based on state budgets. You may lose Medicaid if your annual income goes up. |
| Community and non-profit programs that have subsidized (partly paid) programs for those who do not qualify for Medicaid. | Must meet the requirements of the plan. These vary. | Check with several organizations to find out if you are eligible. Be sure to find out (and get a written explanation) of any amounts you will owe and find out whether this plan will allow you to see the providers you want to see. |
| Through your college/university | Must be enrolled in a college/university that offers health care services. The school may require full-time status before you can be eligible. | Services for certain conditions, especially mental health services, may be limited. On the other hand, you may be able to get many routine services through the student health clinic. |
| Your employer | May need to be employed full-time or work a minimum number of hours each week. | You may be required to have annual screenings or choose from different policy options during the enrollment process. |

## Tips on Applying for Medicaid (Free/Low-cost State Insurance)

Young Adult Road Map Editorial Board Member Shelby Haisley (MSW, LSW, CYC-A) shared some of her personal experiences in the field:

As a service provider for young adults, I have assisted many young adults with applying for health insurance. Here are some "do's" for going through the application process.

- **Do ask for support.** Find someone who has applied for Medicaid before or ask a service provider for help if you have questions. You can also assign someone to be your "**Authorized Representative.**" This means they can call Medicaid on your behalf and receive the same mail you do. This is helpful, especially for your service provider to check on the status of your case.

- **Do turn in any supplemental documents as soon as possible.** Medicaid will send you a letter asking for proof of address, income, etc. Ask your support system for help if needed. Take all documentation to the local Medicaid office. Don't fax it. This way, all your documents will be stamped to show that the office received them on that date.

- **Do keep any stamped, dated documents sent from your local Medicaid office.** If the office loses the originals, you can show you did turn them in on time.

- **Do be patient.** It can take up to three months for your case to be processed. However, if you have questions, go to your local office to get status updates on your case.

- **Do go to your local office to ask questions if you can.** Many offices just have an 800 number, which is automated. You can go to the office and get your questions answered by a real person quicker than being on hold for an hour. The local office also will be more familiar with your case.

- **Do keep all your paperwork!** Medicaid handles many cases and may lose documents or forget to scan them to your electronic file. If they lose your documents, you could lose your insurance coverage.

# Where to Get Medical Care: Consider Your Choices

Where you go for medical help often depends on where you are, the time of day, and what you need. This is an important decision for many young adults as they switch from **pediatric** (children's) services to adult services or start to pay for their own insurance and medical care. For example, if your job or sports team requires a **physical** (an examination of your general health) or a **drug screening examination** (a test to see if you have illegal substances in your body), you may not need to go to a regular physician's office. If you get sick during the weekend when that office is closed, there are other options besides a hospital emergency room. If you need a flu shot, the doctor's office may not be your least expensive choice. Here are some of the main choices and considerations for each choice:

| Medical Care Choice | What this choice offers | What to consider |
|---|---|---|
| "Convenient care" clinics in pharmacies<br><br>• See "Get to Know Your Pharmacist" in Guiding Star Point Four: Manage Information, page 49, for more tips on how pharmacies can help you keep track of medications. | These services can be used on a "walk-in" basis or (in many cases) by appointment. They can be used for drug testing, flu shots, and physicals for work or other activities. Most are open on nights and weekends (but be sure to call or check the store's website). Some clinics allow you to book appointments online. Some systems will automatically text you when you are getting close to the front of the "line" for your appointment, so you won't need to hang around the building. Most convenient care clinics take all major insurance plans, though you may have a co-pay. | The staff may not have access to your records. You may have to fill in a lot of blanks for the staff. Be sure to take your records. If you use these services more than once, try to use the same pharmacy clinic so they keep your records in their system. Even so, you will need to bring your insurance card and ID every time. **NOTE: The walk-in clinic will not have your medication records, even if you use that pharmacy to fill your prescriptions. It is a different system. TAKE YOUR RECORDS.** |
| Health clinic/Health center/ Wellness center at a college or university you attend | Services usually cost no additional fees (outside of your student fees) or are low-cost. This could be a good option for getting an annual flu shot. If you live on campus, this may be the most convenient option if you suddenly feel sick. Campus clinics may also refer you to other services, such as mental health counseling (if these are not provided on campus). | Services may be limited. You may have no choice about which providers you can use. Hours may be limited, especially on smaller campuses. You may have long waiting times for some services during busy times of the year. Check your campus website to see if it's possible to make an appointment online. |

| Medical Care Choice | What this choice offers | What to consider |
|---|---|---|
| Urgent Care ("Walk-In") clinics | These services can be used by walk-in or appointment for non-life-threatening emergencies. They can be used for drug testing and physicals for work or other activities. Many clinics now have equipment for routine X-rays and other tests for injuries. You can see a provider outside of typical business hours. For some walk-in clinics, you can go online to view the types of treatments offered. Walk-in clinics may take your insurance (though you may have a co-pay). | The staff may not have access to your records. You may have to fill in a lot of blanks for the staff. You may have to wait a long time, depending upon the number of people ahead of you and the severity of yours and their situations. However, many clinics now allow you to book appointments online. |
| Regular visits to a family practice physician | You can form a working relationship with the physician or nurse practitioner in a family practice. This practice may take your insurance (though you may have a co-pay). Many practices are in hospitals and will send you to a clinic in the hospital for drug screening and other blood or urine tests. | It may be difficult to get an appointment with the physician for times that work for you and your schedule. If you change insurance plans, check to make sure the practice still takes that insurance and you can afford any co-pay. |
| Free clinic run by community organizations and medical/dental schools | Free treatment, or low-cost treatment (based on your ability to pay). Some clinics offer special services that may not be included in many plans, such as vision and dental services. | Services and hours of operation may be limited. You may have no choice of providers. Services may be offered by less experienced providers, especially at medical/dental schools (although they are supervised by more experienced providers). |
| Nurse practitioner at your family practice office | It is often easier to get an appointment with a nurse practitioner. The nurse practitioner can prescribe medications. You can form a working relationship with the nurse practitioner. The nurse practitioner may work in a practice that will take your insurance plan (be sure to check beforehand). The nurse practitioner may be able to take more time with you than a physician can. | The nurse practitioner is probably not available at night or on weekends. If you suddenly feel sick, you may want to go to a walk-in clinic instead. Certain ailments, like influenza virus ("the flu") can be treated more effectively if you get medical help right away. |
| Emergency room | This service should only be used for a life-threatening emergency or possible major injury (for example, you have been in a car accident and it is not clear if you are seriously injured). Emergency rooms may take your insurance (though you may have a co-pay). | This service can be very expensive. You may sit in a crowded waiting room a long time on busy nights. You have very little control over what services you receive (because you will sign a form agreeing to pay each health provider separately, such as the X-ray tech, doctor, lab tech—before you are given any services). Afterwards, you will probably get bills from multiple providers. Your insurance plan may have a "cap" (maximum amount) it will pay for a visit to an emergency room. |

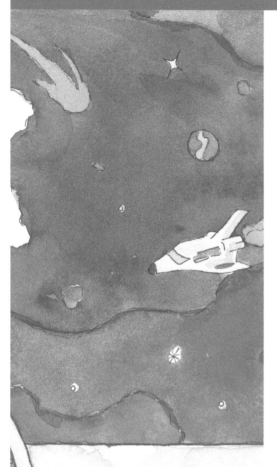

*Even if a behavioral health problem disturbs or upsets someone very much, an emergency room or psychiatric hospital may not be the right choice.*

# Where to Get Behavioral (Mental) Health Care

If you are having a behavioral health problem, what you do next will depend on THREE considerations. (If someone is helping you, you can show them this information.) These considerations are:

1. What is Medically NECESSARY?

2. What is AVAILABLE in your area?

3. What is COVERED by your insurance plan?

(See the glossary for the definition of behavioral health, also called mental health.)

## 1. What is Medically NECESSARY?

Different types of behavioral health problems are treated in different ways. Not every problem—even disturbing issues that may upset you very much—requires a trip to the emergency room or psychiatric hospital. In fact, this may be the wrong choice for getting the services you need. Medically necessary are two very important key words that mean the services are required to treat your symptoms.

Types of behavioral health services are grouped in 12 major treatment categories. This is called the continuum of care.

### Office or outpatient clinic
Visits are usually 30-60 minutes. The number of visits per month depends on the patient's needs.

### Intensive case management
Specially trained individuals coordinate or provide psychiatric, financial, legal, and medical services to help the adolescent or young adult live successfully at home and in the community.

### Home-based treatment services
A team of specially trained staff go into a home and develop a treatment program to help the youth and family or young adult.

### Family support services
These services, such as parent training, parent support group, etc., help families care for their youth or young adult.

### Day treatment program
This intensive treatment program provides psychiatric treatment with special education for school age youth and may provide treatment with other programming for young adults.

### Partial hospitalization (day hospital)
This type of hospitalization provides all the treatment services of a psychiatric hospital, but the patients go home each evening.

### Emergency/crisis services
24-hour-per-day services are available for emergencies (for example, hospital emergency room, mobile crisis team).

### Respite care services
A patient stays briefly away from home with specially trained individuals.

### Therapeutic group home or community residence

This therapeutic program usually includes six to ten persons per home and may be linked with a day treatment program or specialized educational program.

### Crisis residence

This setting provides short-term (usually fewer than 15 days) crisis intervention and treatment. Patients receive 24-hour-per-day supervision.

### Residential treatment facility

Seriously disturbed patients receive intensive and comprehensive psychiatric treatment in a campus-like setting on a long-term basis.

### Hospital treatment

Patients receive comprehensive psychiatric treatment in a hospital. Treatment programs should be specifically designed for either adolescents or adults. Length of treatment depends on different variables.

*Adapted from "Facts for Families: Continuum of Care for Children and Adolescents" fact sheet with permission from the American Academy of Child and Adolescent Psychiatry. For this and other fact sheets, go to http://aacap.org*

## 2. What's Available?

Not all programs and services can be found within every community. However, if your providers can show this service (such as a residential treatment center) is medically necessary, you may be able to go outside your area. You may need to get a letter from your physician to the insurance company as evidence (usually sending records of some kind) to show this is necessary. Call the number on the back of your insurance card and ask what needs to be done. Often, the staff in the physician's or other specialist's office will help with this, but you may need to get involved.

## 3. What's Covered?

Health insurance pays for treatment that is medically necessary. You may have to pay for parts of the coverage, and you may have limits on that coverage (See "Piecing Together the Insurance Puzzle" page 23).

Here are some details that may be important if you have an illness that involves big expenses, such as treatment in a hospital or residential center:

Your plan may also have an annual out-of-pocket maximum, which is the highest amount of deductible and co-payment charges you are expected to pay in one year. An annual or lifetime maximum benefit is the most the insurance company will pay for a treatment over one year or during the whole time you are covered by that plan. You can find all that information on the insurance company's website by looking at the member's handbook. It may be faster than calling for information.

*NOTE:* In public health plans, co-payments and annual maximums may be based on your family income.

You may be able to use something called flexible benefits in your plan to pay for a treatment (such as a residential treatment center) that is not covered by your plan or available in your area.

## DON'T WAIT

If you ever think you are in immediate danger of causing harm to yourself or others, GET HELP right away. Call (or ask someone to call) 911 or a Mobile Crisis number. (You can search "Mobile Crisis near me" or on your phone or other device. (Be aware that the first results to come up may be ads for treatment centers.) You can also search "Statewide Crisis Lines Near Me" or "Statewide Crisis Line (your state)." You can also call the National Suicide Prevention Lifeline (1-800-273-8255), which "provides 24/7, free and confidential support for people in distress, prevention, and crisis resources for you and your loved ones."

*The best way to get results from customer service departments is to keep a log of "who said what and when."*

## INSIDE ADVICE

One insurance company executive recommends that when the customer service associate says, "If you have any problems, just call the main number," you should ask to speak to somebody local. If that doesn't work, ask for a supervisor who can explain the decision. "If you still don't understand, ask to talk to that person's supervisor," the executive suggests. Be persistent. If you have an issue with the person on the phone, ask for that person's company ID number. Put this number in your phone log.

"You need to find someone in the organization who can help you identify the issues and get to solutions," the insurance executive urges. "Keep asking: "What are my rights? What are my options? Keep pushing to get the services you feel you need."

## Use Your Card

If you have a question about your coverage and can't find the answer online, the best thing to do is to call the number on the back of your card. Ask "What are my options?" and "Who can help me with this problem?"

NOTE: If there is a separate number on the card for MH/SA, that stands for Mental Health/Substance Abuse. Call that number instead of the main number.

## Check Out the Choices

You can find out which treatment programs and services are available in your community by looking at the websites of **Community Mental Health Agencies**, hospitals, and other health systems in your area. You can call the main number to ask about services, or have information sent to you by mail (or, in some cases, email). Your state or local NAMI affiliate may also have this information. Call NAMI's national helpline, 800-950-6264, or visit https://nami.org to find the nearest affiliate. Other good sources of help for any mental health need for youth and young adults are state chapters of the National Federation of Families for Children's Mental Health. To find one near you, go to http://ffcmh.org .

## Keep A Phone Log

The best way to get results from customer service departments is to keep a log of "who said what and when." This creates a record of your conversations if you need to go up the chain to a higher authority or file an appeal. It also helps you keep track of issues, so you can explain the problem to the next person. ("My log shows that during June, I made four calls to customer service about approving in-network benefits for this treatment. On the first call, Andrew told me...but on the next call with Amy, I was told....") Frankly, even mentioning that you are writing this down in your phone log helps to get results.

## Find a Guide with Two Names

Your path to solving problems can be very different, depending on whether you have public or private health insurance. If you have public insurance, state law may require that you automatically get assigned to a **case manager** or be assigned one if you ask. In that case, the state has certain agencies you can call with specific problems. The state often pays private **advocacy organizations** to provide certain kinds of help. Look at the back of your insurance card for information. On the other hand, if you have private-pay benefits, you don't get a case manager unless you have a specific problem. You will usually have to ask for this help, and you may even have to insist on getting it.

Here is a common example of what happens when you call an insurance company with a difficult issue:

- Let's say you have a problem getting your private insurance benefits to pay for a treatment from an out-of-network doctor. When you call the helpline number on your card, you will probably have to go through an automated "menu" of selections.

- Finally, you reach a **customer service representative** (customer service associate) who will answer with a first name only. ("Hello, this is Andrew, how may I help you?") This employee is trained to look in your computer file, answer basic questions, and clear up routine errors.

- Andrew quickly realizes that your problem falls outside those basic guidelines. He puts you on hold with recorded music and finds a supervisor.

- The supervisor tells Andrew–and Andrew tells you–that your provider needs to send in a letter with three pieces of information (we'll call them Info A, B, and C). Andrew makes notes about this solution in your computer file. "If you have any other problems," Andrew says cheerfully, "just call the main number and any representative can help you. It's all in the file."

- If you're lucky, that's the end of it.

- If you're not lucky, you must call back again and go through the same automated system to reach a human voice.

- This time, a different person takes the call–let's call her Amy–who needs to hear the whole story again. She looks in your computer file to see what Andrew noted last time.

- Amy tells you Andrew was quite mistaken, because the rules clearly ask for Info D, E, and F. Just to be sure, Amy talks to her supervisor while you listen to more music.

- Eventually, Amy and her supervisor decide—guess what?—the provider should have sent Info A and Info D in the first place.

- You call your provider's office to report this. It turns out the office manager sent Info A and Info D two weeks ago, but nothing happened. So, you call the customer service number and it all begins again….

- When the issue is complicated, you won't get far by dealing with a "first-name-only" phone person. BHOs have special case managers, often called **care managers**, who handle these situations. (Even better are **field care managers**, who are assigned to your local community and understand the regional resources in your area.) A care manager tends to have more power to get things done and will usually give you BOTH his or her first and last names, plus a direct number. This person can be a huge help in breaking through barriers and finding what you need! Still, the path can be long and complicated.

✳ **See Activity 2.1, Medical and Insurance Terms Matching Game**

## SUICIDE AND VIOLENCE RISK

If you know someone who shows any of these signs:

· Sudden change in personality

· Gives away many favorite possessions

· Talks of wanting to die or "disappear"

· Takes unusual risks or shows reckless behavior

· Threatens suicide or violence

· Talks of family or others being "better off without me"

· Has a sudden and frequent interest in death or methods of dying

· Collects objects that may cause harm to self or others

TAKE IT SERIOUSLY. DO NOT DELAY. If you are in school, tell someone in a position of authority, such as a teacher or counselor. If you are at work, tell your supervisor. If this is a friend, try to get that person to seek help (so long as doing this will not put you in any danger. If you think this may happen, tell someone else.)

IF YOU SEE SOMETHING, SAY SOMETHING.

## YOUTH MENTAL HEALTH FIRST AID

Youth Mental Health First Aid is an excellent program that teaches youth/young adults and others to recognize the signs of mental health problems and help people (or themselves) get the support they need. Find out more about this class at https://www.mentalhealth-firstaid.org/take-a-course/course-types/youth/.

## YOU ARE HERE:

# Guiding Star Point Two Review

To find help with your concerns, you may need to talk with people in one or more systems. To find the right people, you will need to learn some of the language used in each system and how things typically get done.

Every system has "key words" that people use to exchange important information and decide whether someone is eligible to get services. (You will find many of those key words and definitions in the Glossary section of this Guide.)

1. Understanding yourself starts with a **physical examination** by a **primary care provider**, who maybe a medical doctor (MD) or a nurse practitioner (NP).

   · This provider may do tests or ask questions about your **behavior**, emotions, or **development**. If there seems to be a problem, he/she may refer you to a **medical specialist** or **behavioral health specialist**.

   · Be sure to bring your **physical examination records** to any specialists who **evaluate** or treat you, since these providers may not do full examinations themselves.

2. Always take your insurance card and some form of "Picture ID" (a driver's license or other state-issued identification) to any appointment.

3. Tell providers what you have observed about yourself, what you think, and what you feel. ***You are the expert about yourself.***

4. Learning key words, including the four basic parts of a **health insurance policy/plan**, can help you talk to people about your choices. You can avoid getting stuck with insurance that costs too much or doesn't pay for the services you need.

5. When you feel sick or get injured, choose the type of medical provider that matches your needs. (For example, you need services to cost under X amount of money, and you need medical help within X amount time.) An emergency room is usually not the best choice.

6. If you have a **behavioral health** issue (problems with thoughts, feelings, emotions, or behavior), the services you receive will depend on (1) what your providers determine is **medically necessary**, (2) what is covered by your insurance plan, and (3) what is available in your community. If you don't agree with a provider's or insurer's decision about what is medically necessary or what should be covered, ask for an explanation. Keep asking if you don't understand. In some cases, these decisions can be changed.

7. If you have a question about your insurance coverage and can't find the answer online, the best thing to do is to call the number on the back of your insurance card. When you call the insurance company, ask "What are my options?" and "Who can help me with this problem?"

8. The best way to get results from customer service departments is to keep a log of "who said what and when." This creates a record of your conversations, which may help if/when you need to go up the chain to a higher authority or file an appeal. It also helps you keep track of issues, so you can explain the problem to the next person.

**YOU ARE HERE**

GUIDING STAR
POINT THREE:

# Build
# Relationships

Communicate your priorities clearly. Show you
expect to be included in all decisions as a
full partner. Find people who can help you
meet goals and solve problems.

## SYSTEM RELATIONSHIPS

We tend to think of **relationships** as social. In this Guide, we talk about the relationships that enable you to get the services you need (relationships with case managers, doctors, therapists, and friends and family members who can support you in **navigating systems**).

*"Life is short. Being a jerk is just unnecessary.... Most good relationships are built on mutual trust and respect."*

*– Mona Sutphen, Former Deputy White House Chief of Staff for Policy*

## Why Build Relationships?

Each time you walk into a room with a provider, remember: As the client, YOU are in a position of authority, too. You and the provider each have a **role** (job) in that room. A provider is trained to be an expert about some part of the system you are trying to navigate. ***You are the expert about yourself.*** Sometimes you will have to *change the conversation* so providers (and others who may be involved in your services, such as families and mentors) accept your role.

In fact, navigating a system has a lot in common with taking part in a **role-playing game.** At different points along the journey, there may be "gatekeepers" (people in charge of getting you into systems or services you need). You may need to build partnerships with people who can tell you how to solve problems or get past barriers. The way you speak and behave toward those people tells them what you expect from them, and what they can expect from you. You may encounter some of these people once or twice, and work with others for years to come. One provider may write something in a file or say something that affects how the next provider treats you. Building relationships of mutual trust and respect can help you get the services and supports you need.

## Working with Providers

Below are some good ideas used by real people who face some of the same challenges you face:

1. **You have a right to be treated with courtesy and respect.** Everyone responds better when they are treated respectfully. If you are over 18, it is not acceptable for you to be treated as less than an equal in making decisions about your services. If you are under 18, you still have a right to be consulted (and in some cases, a right to refuse or consent to treatment).

2. **If you don't understand something, ask for an explanation.** Continue to ask questions until you understand the provider's thinking. You may disagree with providers about their recommendations. Don't be afraid to say so. Providers aren't perfect. Sometimes they are mistaken. If you think what they're suggesting won't work for you, say so. Based on your input, providers may change their recommendations. Effective questions tend to begin with words such as "who, what, when, where, why, how," or "can you please explain?" Asking effective questions is a way to get more information from providers.

3. **Consider your learning style.** Do you take in information better by seeing it or hearing it? You may need to ask for more written material or ask the provider to recommend some videos to explain a situation.

4. **Explain your point of view in a calm, courteous way.** Don't attack the provider just because you don't agree. If you are calm rather than angry when expressing your opinion, the provider will be much more likely to see you as a partner who has a different point

of view rather than as a difficult client. It's okay to disagree, but if you are feeling out of control, ask for a short break to gather yourself. You might also end the session early and schedule another meeting.

5. **If you need more time with the provider, say so.** If your appointment isn't long enough to get all your questions answered, the provider should be willing to schedule more time to meet with you. You are entitled to this. It may mean having to set another meeting on another day, but you have a right to get complete, clear information.

6. **Keep in regular contact with any provider.** In some instances, it's important to see a provider on a regular basis if you are going to get the best care for yourself. Check with providers to see how often they recommend that you talk to them. Find out how they wish to be contacted if something important happens between appointments.

7. **If you are pleased with a provider, say so.** Just like everyone else, providers like to know when they are doing a good job. A simple "thank you" or "I appreciate that" can go a long way toward building a good relationship.

8. **If you can't work things out with a provider directly, you may need to discuss your problems with a supervisor.** Make sure you've made every effort to resolve things with the provider before you see a supervisor. (See "What to Do if Someone's Not Listening," page 40.")

9. **If you have tried all the above and still cannot work with the provider, think about changing to a different person.** Sometimes people and providers simply cannot get along. If you have done the best you can and still do not feel comfortable with the provider, you'll be better off finding someone else to help you. Before you move to a new provider, take a moment to reflect on what happened in the previous situation. When, where, how, and why did communication break down?

10. **Ask about other choices.** For example, some areas don't have many psychiatrists, but you may be able to see a psychiatric nurse practitioner (who often spends more time with each client). Consider the other health care choices you may have. For example, there could be online help or video conferencing (sometimes called **telemedicine**) available to meet your needs. Just as you would do for an office visit, screen the provider for quality.

11. **As a young adult, you have a right to make new choices if you wish to do so.** Even if you have worked with a provider for a long time, it is your choice whether to continue working with them. You have changing needs, and it is important that you are being treated like an adult.

## NVRL8

Be on time for appointments. If you must cancel, give 24 hours' notice whenever possible. Some offices charge for appointments that are cancelled without notice, and insurance companies don't pay for that charge. Take along the office number. If you are stuck in traffic and have a cell phone, call and tell them the reason you might be late. Most offices will give you a 15-minute "grace period." If you are later than this, they may ask you to reschedule.

## Speaking Respectfully vs. Getting Respect

The habit of speaking respectfully to others can be a big strength. However, for young adults who wish to be treated as equal partners in systems, it can be important to use words that "cue" others to respond with equal respect. An example: While it may be polite to say, "yes, sir" and "no, ma'am" to older adults within your culture, sometimes overuse of these phrases can make a provider—especially someone from a different culture—automatically treat you as a person of lower status. It may depend on the system and the situation. This is something you must "feel out" for yourself. However, it can help to get advice from a trained peer support worker, or to observe others in your situation who seem to be successful in navigating that system. In any case, never use words that disrespect yourself, such as "I don't know much, but...." or "This may be a stupid question, but...." *You are the expert about yourself*, and your questions always deserve respect.

## USING THE REFLECTIVE RESPONSE

When talking with someone during an appointment, it helps to summarize what you hear. This is also called using a "Reflective Response" because you are holding up a kind of mirror that reflects the words back to the provider. You can say things such as:

*"In other words, are you saying...."*

*"So, do you mean...."*

*"Do I understand correctly that..."*

*"Let me just be sure I have this right..."*

*"So, what I hear you saying is...."*

When you use a Reflective Response, the provider can correct any misunderstanding or add more information if necessary. (It also makes it easier for you to remember what was said.)

## Getting Your Medical Provider's Full Attention

Change the conversation

Medical office schedules are designed to move patients in and out very quickly. Doctors may spend most of the appointment looking at your electronic medical records on a screen and interrupt what you're saying to ask questions. They may offer a solution and leave the room before you remembered to tell what you need them to hear or ask everything you need to know. This can feel frustrating—and you may not get the best medical care. You can *change the conversation* by showing you expect to be an equal partner in treatment. Here's how:

- **Prioritize concerns.** Come prepared to explain your top three concerns for that appointment. (This is good advice for any appointment.) See "Making the Most of Appointment Time." To practice developing priority concerns, use Activity 1.2, What are My Concerns?

✳ **See Activity 1.2, What Are My Concerns?**

- **Tell the story. Explain why you have these concerns.** This offers more information, so the medical provider is less likely to interrupt you with questions. For example, instead of saying "my shoulder hurts," you might say, "I fell playing soccer a week ago, the coach iced my shoulder to keep it from swelling, but it seems worse, and I feel a sharp pain in front when I move it."

- **Bring a written, numbered list of questions.** Providers pay more attention when you pull out a list of questions (on paper or your phone) and say something such as "I have five questions." The magic here is pulling out the paper/phone and mentioning numbers. These provide "cues" to a provider to slow down and listen.

- **Ask questions about treatment and next steps.** Before the provider leaves the room, ask any questions about the recommended treatment and what will happen next. Make sure you understand details about any follow-up appointments, and you know what to do if you have any problems with the treatment. Ask for written information if you need it. Ask what to do if you think of more questions later. Before you leave, do an "exit check." Make sure the provider has given you all necessary copies of prescriptions sent electronically, plus medicine samples, instructions, and paperwork.

- **If you still can't get the provider's attention, consider changing providers.** You have a right to be heard and get full information, so you can make the best decisions about your own care. If your choice of medical providers is limited (for example, you get care from a free or low-cost clinic and don't always see the same person), you may need to advocate in a different way. See "What to Do if Someone's Not Listening" on page 40.

## Avoiding Common System Errors

Sometimes important lab results don't show up before your next appointment. The **referral** doesn't go through. The insurance paperwork has the wrong **number code**. A phone message gets mangled on its way between offices. Human errors will always happen, but a few tricks can help the information get where it needs to go.

**One rule of thumb: If you can cut out a step that somebody else normally does, you can cut down the number of times it gets done wrong.** Example: On some health forms and laboratory paperwork, you are asked to list doctors or other providers who should be informed. Make sure to have the names and contact information for providers who should get copies. If office staff members must look up the information, the task may get put on the "hold" pile until someone has spare time. Next, find out when the results will be ready. If the doctor needs them soon, call the office on that day to see if the results have been received. If the results have not shown up, your call will remind the staff to call and ask the lab about them. Before your next visit, check to see if the test results have arrived.

Often there is only space for two or three names on that list of contacts, and sometimes the office will send results only to specialists involved in your care. (Remember, they may not be able to send your records to other providers without a signed **release form** from you.)

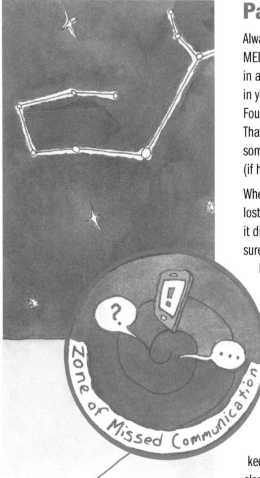

## Passing Notes, Patient Portals

Always ask for a copy of any report or lab result. YOU HAVE A RIGHT TO GET A COPY OF YOUR MEDICAL DOCUMENTS. Offices now use **electronic medical records** (medical records stored in a computer), but staff should be willing to make you a paper copy. Save this paper copy in your binder. (Find out more about keeping a binder for your records in Guiding Star Point Four, "Manage Information.") Many people now keep records on their tablets or phones. That is your choice, but paper is always a safe backup when technology fails! If there is something in this report that another team member should know, write a note or email (if he or she is a provider) to put the information in your file.

Whenever possible, WRITE the information--don't just tell it to the person. Information gets lost, forgotten, or misunderstood. Plus, you may need a record later. If it is not documented, it didn't happen. Email is best because you have a record of what you wrote. If you are not sure about what to include, ask the provider to help you before you leave the appointment. If writing is difficult for you, find out if you can get a case manager or an advocate from a local organization to help you. Try calling 211 on the phone or visit 211.org online to ask about resources to help young adults with special physical, mental health, or developmental needs.

Many health providers now use a **patient portal** to keep records and exchange information with patients and family caregivers. In this system, you can sign into a personal account that allows you to find information, set up or cancel appointments, and send messages to your health provider. If your pediatrician or other health provider offers this system, sign up. If it seems confusing, ask someone in the provider's office to help you during the next appointment. This is one more reason to keep a good relationship with provider support staff! They usually know better than anyone else how their systems work.

*Whenever possible, WRITE information, don't just tell it. Information gets lost, forgotten, or misunderstood. Plus, you may need a record later.*

## Good Questions About Medication

1. Should I check in with your office before the next appointment to let you know how the medication is working? If so, when and how?

2. How shall I contact you about a side effect that worries me? (Tip: Write down the phone number and a contact name. Ask if there is a "patient portal," which is an online way to contact your provider's office and/or keep medical records.)

3. If you are not available, whom should I call or contact? Ask for contact information.

Don't forget to WRITE DOWN the answers.

# Tips for Sending Updates

Updates can be sent by phone, email, or text. Ask your provider which method is best for him or her. Many offices use patient portals, but in some cases, a provider might want you to text or call (for example, if a certain side effect occurs, or you have an urgent need for help).

An update note doesn't have to be formal or complicated. The important points to include:

- Key facts (what happened and/or changed, such as a medication change, treatment plan change, etc.)
- Your date of birth (one way the provider's office retrieves your records from their files)
- Date(s) this happened
- Who is involved (for example, what provider made the change) and this person's role
- What paperwork is included with this note, if any (such as a lab or test result)
- Any additional information
- Where you can be reached (phone number and/or email) if a release form is needed

If you are sending this note to a provider, it helps to add: "Please include this information in my file and contact me if you need further information. Thank you for helping to keep my records up to date."

### For a MEDICATION CHANGE, tell:

Other doctors

Therapists

Case Manager

Representatives of agencies (example: probation officer, peer coach, wellness coach....)

Trusted people (friends, mentors, family members)

### For a TREATMENT PLAN CHANGE, tell:

All doctors

Other therapists

Trusted people

### For a MAJOR LIFE EVENT (such as a trauma), tell:

Employer (if going to be away from work)

Doctors

Therapists

Representatives of agencies

Trusted people

## FORMS, FORMS, FORMS

The Health Insurance Portability and Accountability Act (HIPAA) requires health providers to get your consent before releasing information under certain conditions. In general, you will have to sign a release every time information is sent from one organization (such as your doctor's office) to another organization (such as the insurance plan administrators). If you don't understand who will get this information and for what reason, don't sign until you get the answers.

Make sure you understand what will be sent to other providers. In some cases, providers will send all the details in your records. In other cases, providers may summarize information.

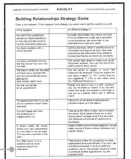

✳ **See Activity 3.1, Building Relationships Strategy Game**

## GETTING HELP FROM ADVOCACY GROUPS

**Family advocacy organizations** can help with advice or letter-writing. In some cases, a member of an organization will go with you to a meeting or appointment. One of the most useful family advocacy organizations is the National Alliance on Mental Illness (NAMI), which has affiliate groups all over the nation. Many NAMI affiliates also offer free classes and support groups. Go to http://nami.org to find the closest affiliate.

Another excellent source of help are chapters of the National Federation of Families for Children's Mental Health. Go to http://ffcmh.org to find one near you.

Oasis of Peer Support

## What to Do When Someone's Not Listening

Sometimes, no matter what you do, a relationship isn't working. However, it is not always easy to switch to a new person in certain agencies or clinics. You may have limited choices. There are still ways to navigate the situation. Here are five strategies that may help:

1. If you have a problem with a provider, first talk to him or her about it before going to someone higher up in the agency. Listen to the provider, and politely insist the provider listen to you. If the problem is resolved, thank the provider. If you are not satisfied, take your concern to the next level by asking to speak with a supervisor. Ask to speak with a person higher up if necessary.

2. If you are still not satisfied, file a **grievance** (written complaint) with the agency, government authority, or **behavioral health organization**. You can usually learn about grievance procedures by going to the agency's website. You can also ask a family advocacy agency to help you. (Note: In most states, there are special agencies that help people with complaints about state health insurance/Medicaid.)

3. In your **complaint** (written statement of what happened) include dates, names of those involved, witnesses, and specific details. Stick to the facts. Write what happened, not what you think or feel about what happened.

4. If your complaint involves serious wrongdoing by the provider (such as anything that may be a crime or cause you serious physical or emotional harm), do not wait. Report this to a trusted person and the provider's supervisor immediately. Give details, including the day, time, and facts concerning what was said and done. Write down these details. Also write down the name or names of those you informed about this incident, along with the date and time.

5. If something didn't work out with a provider, take some time afterwards to think about or discuss with someone: What went wrong? Did I have other options? Is there some other strategy I might want to use next time?

# Practicing Assertiveness

The way you speak, move, dress, and react can affect how you are treated by providers. Assertiveness experts offer these tips on getting results at an appointment or meeting:

- Project the right image.

- Dress neatly.

- Shake hands firmly. Make strong eye contact.

- Take time to organize records and paperwork.

- Sit or stand in an upright but relaxed way. Keep your body still and relaxed. Fidgeting will make you seem uneasy or lacking in confidence.

- If you feel nervous, practice what you want to say ahead of time.

- Speak with confidence.

- State clearly and calmly what you believe to be true ("I think that... I feel that...").

- Speak up in a strong tone of voice without asking for permission or making apologies.

- Don't try to attack, bully, blame, or shame the other person. Your goal is to solve problems, not win arguments.

- Listen to the other person carefully. Show you are listening by wearing an alert, attentive expression.

- Refer to the other person's point of view when you give a different opinion ("I understand that you feel...,but I believe...").

- When you honestly agree with the person, say so. A little stroking never hurts ("Yes, that seems like a good idea.").

- Don't raise your voice. If you aren't satisfied, say so politely but firmly. Make suggestions. Ask for ideas.

- Do NOT text while talking with others. It makes you look like you are avoiding the conversation or not paying attention.

## Show you expect results

- Before you leave the room, briefly sum up the discussion, describing what each person has agreed to do (action items) in a certain amount of time. Follow up on those items in the agreed upon time.

- State decisions in terms of "we" and "us" ("So, as I understand it, we've decided to..."). Remember, you are the other vote in the room.

- If you think the other person may not clearly understand or stick to the agreement, send a note that sums up the decisions made in your meeting, or get a person you trust to help you with this, if necessary. Keep a copy for your files. In case of a conflict, this letter becomes part of the record to help you get results.

# LGBTQI2-S

Some young adults who identify as **Lesbian, Gay, Bisexual, Transgender, Queer/Questioning, Intersex, or 2-Spirited (LGBTQI2-S)** face special challenges when they look for medical or behavioral health care. They may feel uncomfortable talking with certain providers about **gender orientation** or **sexuality** issues. Medical doctors and nurses may have little or no training about how to serve **gender non-conforming** patients. The issues get more complicated for underage teens who worry that a doctor might "out" them to family members. (In many cases, doctors and nurses keep this information **confidential** unless there is reason to suspect the patient will be harmed or will harm someone else. However, that is NOT always true. To be sure, ask: "Will the health information I give you be shared with my family?")

Look for providers who have experience with LGBTQI2-S clients. "I recommend connecting with local **advocacy organizations**," says Jasmine Marshall, a young social worker in Chicago who is active in the LGBTQI2-S community. "Usually, the best treatment providers are the ones that the local community itself recommends."

Some helpful national resources include: National Youth Advocacy Coalition http://nyacyouth.org and Gay, Lesbian and Straight Education Network https://www.glsen.org/ Both offer excellent blog and other information contributed by young adults. Another source of information about choosing providers for the transgender and intersex community is Rad Remedy Transgender Health Network (University of California) http://radremedy.org/resource/2526/

## YOU ARE HERE:

## Guiding Star Point Three Review

To find help with your concerns, you may need to talk with people in one or more systems. To find the right people, you will need to learn some of the language used in each system and how things typically get done.

Every system has **key words** that people use to exchange important information and decide whether someone is eligible to get services. (You will find many of those key words and definitions in the Glossary section of this Guide.)

1. As the client, you are in a position of authority and have a right to be treated with respect. Sometimes you have to *change the conversation* about your role by speaking and behaving in ways that show you expect to be a full partner in decisions about your services.

2. Be prepared for appointments. Arrive on time. Explain your top three concerns or reasons for being there. Bring a written, numbered list of any questions you may have. Look directly at the provider when speaking or listening. Don't text or view social media on your phone during this time.

3. Use the "Reflective Response." This means repeating the basic points of what the provider said. It allows the provider to clear up any misunderstanding or add more information.

4. Keep in touch with providers between visits. Ask providers how they want to be contacted if something changes. Use **patient portals** if they are available. Communicate in writing whenever you can. When calling or sending a note to a provider about some change that affects your services, include your date of birth, full name, contact information, and the date of the event.

5. State clearly and calmly what you believe to be true. Use "I" statements such as "I think that…." and "I feel that…." Don't raise your voice. If you aren't satisfied, say so politely but firmly. Make suggestions. Ask for ideas.

Speak your mind,
even if your
voice shakes.

– Maggie Kuhn, Social Activist

GUIDING STAR
POINT FOUR:
# Manage Information

Keep good records. Track and report your progress so medical providers and others can understand how you are doing. Insist on clear explanations of any evaluations or reports that are used to make decisions about you.

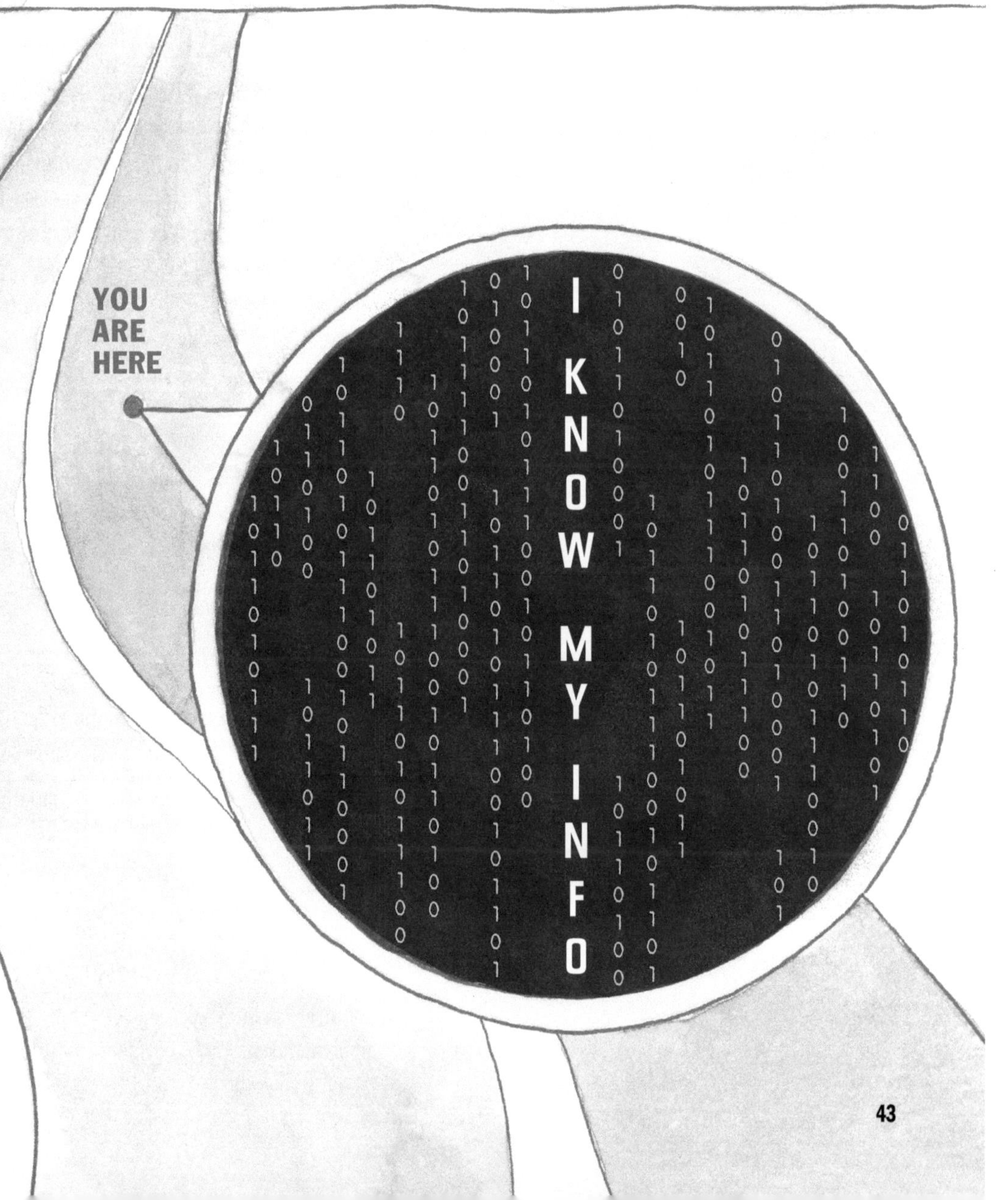

YOU
ARE
HERE

I KNOW MY INFO

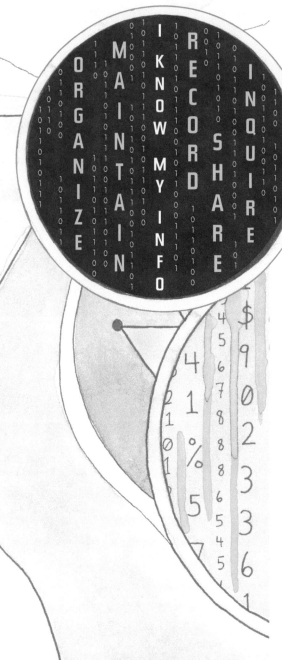

## Why Manage Information?

There's you, and there's "you on file." As you navigate systems, countless pieces of personal information travel along with you. Some pieces are used to decide whether you are eligible (allowed to get services) for programs. Information about your behavior and concerns may be used to recommend treatment for you. Some pieces determine whether insurance will pay for treatment. However, the providers who make those decisions and recommendations see only parts of your information at certain points in time. For example, a medication management visit with a psychiatrist or nurse practitioner may be scheduled for 15 minutes every few weeks. A physical therapy session may be less than an hour once per week. None of these providers can see what's happening when you go home. Even with electronic records, they may not know what other services you receive or what other providers tried when you were younger. They need you to bring them complete and accurate information, so they can offer the right solutions.

## Information Tells Your Story

If you received services as a child, someone had to keep track of your assessments, treatments, educational programs, and benefits. Living as an independent adult means learning to manage your own personal information. Here's one reason managing your own health information is so important: **The facts in your files tell a story about you.** You may need to use that personal information to *change the conversation* about whether you can get services (or get something paid for by your insurance plan). You may need to use your information to show people what happened in the past so mistakes aren't made. Information from a transition plan may show "The Big Picture" of what you want for your everyday life. (See page 11 in this Guide for more about "The Big Picture.") You may need to ask for clear explanations of information in your personal file, such as test scores or lab results, so you can be an equal partner in making treatment decisions. As an independent adult with your own voice, **managing your own information means taking charge of your story**. Although it may sound complicated to keep track of forms and details, there are simple strategies for pulling it all together.

As your own information manager, you have five tasks:

1. **Organize:** Keep your personal data organized and accurate, so you can find the right pieces of information when you need them.

2. **Maintain:** Take medications (and follow other parts of a treatment plan) in a safe, organized way.

3. **Record:** Observe how treatment and other services affect your daily life.

4. **Share:** Tell providers about treatment progress in an organized way and make sure they have other necessary information.

5. **Inquire:** Ask questions about your medications, test results, and lab results so you understand what the provider is recommending and can make informed decisions about treatment.

# Part One: ORGANIZE

A two-inch, three-ring binder is a good place to keep paperwork organized and available for appointments, phone calls, and anytime you need to check information. You may want to put a cheap, three-hole-punched calendar (often given away free by companies) to record appointments and medication dosages. This can be helpful even if you keep appointments on an electronic calendar because scribbling notes down on a calendar can be a good backup. Try adding tabbed dividers using the following labels: personal data, health provider visits, medications, evaluations, school, and insurance/social agencies.

In the personal data section of your binder, include a copy of your insurance card, birth certificate, and Social Security card or number. You may wish to "three-hole-punch" a standard business envelope, put it in your binder, and place the copy of your Social Security Card or number inside to keep this information secure from identity theft. Add a few sheets of notepaper to each section.

## Give Yourself Some Space

When you go to a health provider's office for the first time, you usually fill out a Health History (a form containing basic information about your health, now and in the past). It can be very nerve-racking to fill out forms in 10 or 15 minutes while sitting in a crowded waiting room. Whenever possible, try to have these forms mailed to you before the appointment, so you can fill them in on your own time. Often, the physician or other provider's office will have the forms available online.

The spaces on these forms are usually tight. If you have more to say, add extra sheets of paper or write on the reverse side. Write "see over" or "see attached notes" on the form and "additional notes about (write your name and date of birth)" on any additional pages, in case they get separated from the other forms when office staff adds your information into electronic medical records. Writing your "DOB" (date of birth) on ANY notes is a good idea because that is one way for the medical office staff to find your files in computer systems.

You can fill out the sample My Health History form (Activity 4.1), and file it in your binder under the "personal data" section. This form will keep your basic information close at hand for when you need to fill out a form for a new provider.

## LABEL IT

Label your binder with your name and the year. At the end of the year, put the binder up on the shelf and start a new binder. This is a convenient way to keep an annual record of your treatment. You may want to add a zipper pouch to the front of your binder to keep small items, such as prescription receipts, appointment cards, or business cards from providers. (Some people like to customize their binders to express their own style. If you want to reuse your binder at the end of the year, you can put your records in a labeled envelope or folder at the end of the year and re-use the binder.)

*If you engage with social media accounts, apps, or RPGs (role-playing games), you probably manage a large amount of information every day.*

✳ **See Activity 4.1, My Health History**

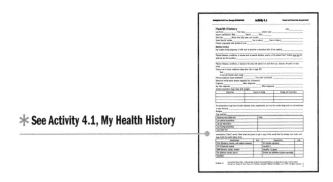

45

## UNDERSTANDING OUR PATHS

Transgenerational trauma is a form of post-traumatic stress disorder that carries over from one generation to the next. It can continue down multiple lines.

When my mother was 10, it was her job to take care of her alcoholic mother and her younger sibling. To cope with the stress of being the head of the family at such a young age, my mother turned to alcohol to numb her feelings about her situation. As a result, my mother grew to be an alcoholic.

When I was 10 years old, my mother, by then a drug addict, couldn't take care of herself or her children. As the eldest child, I took on the responsibility of caring for both her and my younger brother and sister. I was exhausted all the time and trying to succeed in school. To make it easier in this difficult environment, I started taking Adderall, to which I quickly became addicted.

## Family Medical History

Health providers often ask about illnesses in close family members. This is because genetic traits (physical and mental qualities you are born with) can lead to certain illnesses that run-in families. Knowing that an illness has occurred in a close, blood relative may help a doctor determine what's happening to you. In some cases, a medication that is used to treat an illness in one family member may have a better chance to be successful with another family member. Remember that the genetic traits you have inherited are nobody's fault and out of your control. However, they are very important pieces of information that help fill in the picture for you. If you have concerns about who will be able to see your personal information, discuss this with the provider(s) who evaluates and treats you.

## Substance Abuse and Other Behaviors

It is very important that providers who work with you know about anything that can affect your health, behavior, and emotions. That means knowing about family alcohol and drug abuse, sexual abuse, and any unusual family behaviors or traumas (very negative or bad events, such as a death, injury, sexual abuse, or divorce) that you have experienced. In most cases, the provider is required to keep this information confidential (not telling the police, your employer, or others not involved in your treatment) unless the situation could cause a major risk to the safety of you or others. There are exceptions to this rule. If you have any questions, talk to the provider about how the information will be used. If you aren't comfortable listing the information on the forms in this Guide, write it down in a safe place, and don't forget to share it with the provider.

## Part Two: MAINTAIN

For people with special health needs, one of the first steps toward independence is learning to take medications on time, every day, and without prompts from others. Like any skill, this takes practice, and many people need support to keep them safe from mistakes until they develop a regular life routine. If you don't take medications independently yet, you and your family or guardians may want to start a conversation with your provider about how you can begin to gain skills. If you are in middle or high school, learning to take medications independently can be written into your transition goals. (See more about school transition planning in the final chapter of this Guide, "The Bridge to Everywhere," page 63.)

# Avoiding Medication Mix-ups

A good routine is the key to giving medications safely. Here are some "provider approved" strategies for making sure medications stay organized.

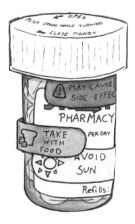

- If you take regular doses of more than one drug, keep these medications sorted in a seven-day pill organizer. Buy this small, inexpensive plastic box at any pharmacy. These boxes are not just for the "mature" crowd. You can see at a glance if a dose has been missed. The organizer makes it much easier to take meds accurately on a busy morning when you are rushing out the door. You can also use app prompts or phone alarms to remind you to take your pills at certain times of the day.

- Put vitamins and other **over-the-counter medicines** (non-prescription medicines) in the same pill organizer as your prescription pills.

- Refill the pill organizer on the same day each week. This is a good time to check the front of the bottle for the number of refills left.

- Don't split pills, unless your doctor/nurse practitioner says this is okay. Some pills cannot be split safely. If you must split pills, buy an inexpensive pill-cutter from the pharmacy. You can also talk with the pharmacist about options for purchasing a different dosage.

- Share information about your medication only with providers, trusted friends, and family.

- In some cases, you may be legally required to leave pills (such as **ADHD** medications) in the original container. If you are involved with a child welfare agency or the court system, be sure to check with a person in charge of your case about the rules for handling your medications.

- Some pharmacies offer pills already sorted into daily "blister packs." They may charge a fee if your insurance does not cover this service.

✳ **See page 80** for a list of common medication abbreviations you may find on prescription forms or in your medical files.

## WHAT TO KNOW ABOUT DRUG WARNINGS

New information about medications is always appearing. Sometimes a drug will be given a **black-box warning** by the FDA, which tells doctors to be careful about prescribing the drug under certain conditions. A black-box warning doesn't necessarily mean the drug is dangerous under all conditions. Sometimes warnings are about not using certain drugs for certain disorders. Sometimes they warn about **drug interactions**, which means possible problems when one drug is used at the same time as another drug. Other warnings are for dangerous side effects that may (but don't always) occur. The website http://medlineplus.gov, a service of the National Library of Medicine and the National Institutes of Health, covers hundreds of medications and health topics.

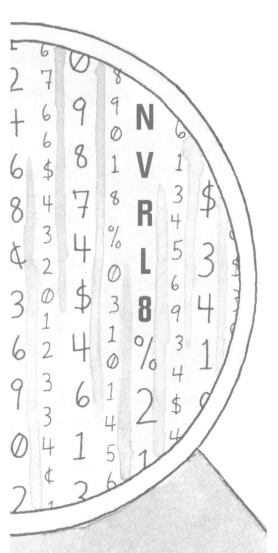

*Various smartphone apps also allow patients to track medication usage. The main thing is to keep it simple and make sure it fits your style.*

## Preventing Confusion About Drug Samples

Sometimes the doctor will **titrate** a new medication (build up from a smaller to a larger dose over a period of days or weeks). This is done to find out what amount works best or to cut down on possible side effects. Some medications need to build up in the body over days or weeks to be effective. In a crisis, a doctor may prescribe an extra medication (for a short time) to keep symptoms under control until another medication has time to build up to a **therapeutic dose**. If a new medication is being tried (especially if the medication is expensive), the provider may start you with free samples. He or she may say something such as, "Take 10 milligrams for the first three days, then raise it to 20 milligrams for a week, then call and let me know how it's going." The trouble is that a sample package does not have your dosage on the label the way a regular prescription would. It's easy to get confused, especially when you are changing the dosage from day to day. Be sure you know the dosage of pills in the sample package.

## Keeping a Titration Record

Ask the provider to write down instructions for titrating medications. If you're getting a prescription, ask the doctor to write titration instructions on the prescription form. This will help to ensure that you get the right number of pills from the pharmacy.

If a medicine is being **titrated** (gradually increased over days or weeks), you will need to keep the dosage straight and observe results. Here is a five-point plan for keeping things straight:

1. An easy method for keeping track of titration doses is to use the inexpensive calendar you put in the front of your binder (see page 45).

2. In each day block, write the medication name and correct dose for that day (example: 5 mg at breakfast, 5 mg before bed).

3. Put a check by the medication name when that dose is taken.

4. At the end of the day or the next day, you can jot down a few words about side effects and results, such as "Less appetite. Got all homework done without prompting."

5. This gives you a simple and accurate day-to-day record of how the medicine worked at different levels. At the next appointment, you can show this calendar page to the doctor.

Various smartphone apps also allow patients to track medication usage. The main thing is to keep it simple and make sure it fits your style.

## Get to Know Your Pharmacist

- **A good pharmacist could be your single best source of information about medications.** Most are willing to spend time making sure you have all the facts. Pharmacists also know a lot about your prescription drug insurance.

- **Use the same pharmacy location each time you fill your prescription(s).** If that's not possible, use the same chain. The stores in one chain will usually use the same computer system to hold patient prescriptions. If your insurance requires you to use a "mail-order" pharmacy, there is usually a toll-free number to call with questions. Ask about automated refill services.

- **Look before you leave.** Look on the bottle or with the packaging that comes with your medications. Always check the label on the medicine bottle to make sure the details match the prescription form. If the doctor sends the information to the pharmacy electronically, without giving you a prescription form, ask for a copy of the form before you leave.

- **Find out about generics.** Pharmacists may substitute the less expensive, "generic" version for a name-brand drug. That's fine so long as the doctor has not marked "name brand only" on the prescription. Also, look at the drug information inside the prescription envelope, medicine box, or flyer.

- **Ask the pharmacist about side effects, even if the doctor has already mentioned them.** A busy doctor may not tell you everything (or know everything) about a medication. Unlike health practices, pharmacies usually can answer questions on nights and weekends and will get right on the phone with you. Often, they can also call doctors' offices directly and get answers more quickly.

## YOUR MEDICATION HISTORY

Use the Medication Log to list your medications. It is okay to make copies of this page for your own use and put those copies in your binder (See Activity 4.2, My Medication Log).

It is VERY important to know what medicines you've taken in the past, as well as the present.

⋆ **See Activity 4.2, My Medication Log**

# Medication Safety Tips

1. **STORE MEDICATIONS AT THE RIGHT TEMPERATURE.** Many drugs are sensitive to heat and may become less effective. Some people keep a small container with extra meds in a purse or car. If so, make sure the meds are securely stored and don't get overheated.

2. **STORE MEDICATIONS IN A SAFE PLACE.** If young children are in the house, use childproof caps.

3. **NEVER** take more or less of a medication than the doctor prescribes.

4. **NEVER** stop taking a medication without talking to the doctor.

5. **ASK THE DOCTOR OR PHARMACIST** what to do if a dose is missed or spit up. Follow these instructions carefully. It may be dangerous or ineffective to take a "make-up" dose.

6. **KNOW WHAT TO DO IN CASE OF AN ACCIDENTAL OVERDOSE.** In a crisis situation, call 911 for help, and ask to be connected to Poison Control for more advice until help arrives.

7. **PREVENT DRUG ABUSE.** Store your medications in a location other than a commonly shared space, especially if you have roommates or company. Medications prescribed to you are for your use only. *Sharing medications prescribed to you is not only dangerous, but it is also illegal in many places.* If the person you share medications with has an adverse reaction, you could be held liable for their condition, i.e., you could be sued and/or face criminal charges.

# Part Three: RECORD

Effective treatment relies on a good **treatment plan** with regular, honest communication between you and the provider. As your own information manager, your tasks are to:

1. Observe how the treatment affects you in everyday life.

2. Keep simple records about what happens, so you can discuss progress with your provider. Many details will be forgotten by the time you get to your next appointment. Your records let you tell a more complete story about what's happening.

3. Watch for any danger signs and take prompt action to get help. This means you should alert your family members or roommates to any negative reaction(s) you feel. They must understand your needs and wishes clearly in case they must communicate with others on your behalf.

For a busy young adult who may be balancing school, work, and just coping in daily life, these tasks can seem impossible. What if you make a mistake with medication? How do you know what side effects to look for? Who has time to write down all the details of your day? What if you just aren't an organized person?

The good news: You don't have to be neat, organized, or any kind of expert to do the tasks listed above. It is most important to have a routine that *FITS YOUR PERSONAL STYLE.* To get them started on a routine or tell help them stay on a routine, some people use lists they check off when they have completed a task. Some people use electronic alarms or electronic prompts. These tools can be especially helpful if you struggle with memory issues.

Everybody functions better when a few things are done the same way every day. Most people are more likely to stick to routines that are simple. Also, as you work through the transition to your adult life, routines help keep you grounded in a predictable, safe reality. When many things are changing, routines can be very comforting. You probably have some of these routines in your life already. Maybe you do certain things when you get up in the morning, right after a meal, or just before bed.

**Some people set routines by using simple checklists. Others may plan tasks by blocks of time (mid morning) or at specific times (9:00 am).**

## How to Be a Good Recorder

The key is to link a record-keeping routine with other natural routines in your life. That way, when the unexpected happens, you are more likely to go back to these tasks.

Let's say you are starting to prepare for the next day. Before you do that, you might use this time to reflect on this day. You pull out your journal or binder (or go to the computer) and make a few notes about the day. Maybe you decide to spend 10 minutes updating some of the worksheets in this chapter. If you update your journal, binder, and/or worksheets every weeknight, that's all the time it takes. If you miss a few nights because something happens, you can go back to these habits when you can return to the regular routine.

Keep your routine simple and short. Give yourself time to get used to it. It's okay if it doesn't always work. Attach the check-in routine to something pleasant, like having a snack, drinking a beverage, or watching a video.

Also, it's a good idea to make sure your binder/pencil/pen/tablet have a regular storage place so you don't have to use your check-in time to hunt for what you need.

You can use the worksheets for Activities 4.3, My Side Effects Log and 4.4, My Behavior Log to make notes you may want to share with a provider. (It's okay to make copies of these pages for your own use. Put copies in your binder.)

See Activities **4.3, My Side Effects Log** and **4.4, My Behavior Log**.

✳ **See Activity 4.3, My Side Effects Log**

✳ **See Activity 4.4, My Behavior Log**

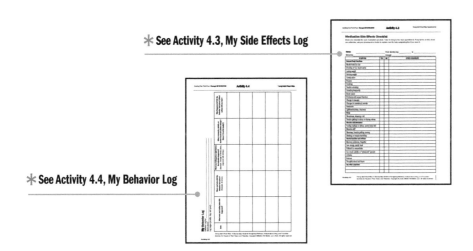

## THREE DIFFERENT WAYS TO ORGANIZE YOUR DAY

| CHECKLIST |
|---|
| Woke up |
| Bathed |
| Brushed teeth |
| Took morning medications |
| Made bed |
| Noted in my journal that I didn't sleep well for the fourth night in a row |

| BLOCKS OF TIME |
|---|
| Early morning |
| Late morning |
| Early afternoon |
| Late afternoon |
| Early evening |
| Late evening |

| TIME OF DAY |
|---|
| 9:00 AM |
| 10:00 AM |
| 11:00 AM |
| 12:00 PM |
| 1:00 PM |
| 2:00 PM |

## DON'T BE EMBARRASSED TO SPEAK UP

Some people find it especially embarrassing or difficult to talk to a doctor or nurse about certain medical conditions, such as:

- Sexually transmitted diseases (STDs), which are diseases spread by sexual contact with others

- Herpes (a type of painful blister on the mouth or sexual organs, spread by contact with others)

- Body odors, including bad breath

- Objects stuck in any part of the body

Medical providers see people with these conditions all the time. They can treat problems before they get worse or cause other issues. Remember, your provider's job is to keep you healthy. Just give the facts and ask about your options for treatment.

## Part Four: SHARE

You can bring the doctor, nurse, or other provider up-to-date by showing the charts mentioned above at each appointment. Keep all the charts for a year in your binder. Without much effort on your part, your provider(s) will have a detailed record of your progress. If you would rather not show your notes to a provider, make a written list of points you want to discuss about your progress. For example, you might want to discuss certain side effects, such as trouble sleeping or loss of appetite. Add any questions to this list. Don't forget to ask about words you don't understand or parts of the **treatment plan** that don't seem clear to you.

Your treatment plan is about you. Honesty with the provider is honesty with yourself. Some people feel shame because they have some form of disability or have experienced some type of **trauma**. Shame becomes another burden to carry around. When it keeps you from being honest with a provider about what's happening during treatment, the power of shame grows. For example, if you think a medication is causing **sexual dysfunction** (difficulty during sexual activities that are typical for you), share that with the provider who prescribes that medication.

Consider: When you look back in your binder, journal, worksheets, or other records of treatment, what differences have occurred since you started the treatment plan? Do your friends and family notice differences? These details should also be part of your record.

### Keeping an Eye on "The Big Picture"

Even the best providers can sometimes lose track of "The Big Picture" of what you want for your everyday life as an independent adult. As you share your treatment progress, think about whether the goals in your plan are being met. If something bothers you, ask questions. Do these goals still make sense based on what YOU have observed about yourself at this point in time? If not, you may need to *change the conversation*. Treatment plans are "living documents" that can be changed as needed. If you don't know how to start that conversation, it's always a good idea to make a list of your strengths and concerns. Does the treatment plan make use of your strengths? Does it address your most important concerns right now? Consider asking a trusted person to look over this list and help you plan questions to discuss with your provider.

# Part Five: INQUIRE

As an adult, you want to have a voice in any decisions about your treatment. To do that, you need to understand the basic facts about medications and tests that are part of your treatment. Tests may be behavioral (such as a test for symptoms of depression) or medical (such as a urine test for signs of physical illness). You may also need to have regular medical ("lab") tests if you are taking certain psychiatric medications that need to be monitored (watched) for any effect on your physical health.

*The art and science of asking questions is the source of all knowledge.*

*– Thomas Berger, Novelist*

**Good questions to ask about your medication:**

- What if I can't swallow a pill or capsule? Is it available in chewable or liquid form? Can a pill be cut in half?

- What is the dosage? Is it likely to change during the time I am getting used to it?

- Is there a less expensive, generic version I can take?

- Do I need to avoid any foods when taking this medication?

- What are possible side effects? Which ones are most likely?

- Which side effects mean that I should contact your office immediately?

- What if I skip a dose or throw up the medication?

- How many times each day must the medicine be taken? What time of day?

- Does this medication need to be taken with food?

- Will I need to take any regular "lab" tests to monitor this medication?

**Good questions to ask about medical and behavioral tests:**

- What is the name of the test?

- Why am I being given this test?

- What other tests are available? What other tests should we consider?

- What kinds of information will this test provide?

- When will this test be given?

- Can I eat or drink before this test?

- How long will the test take?

- Who will administer (give) the test to me?

- When and how (mail, email, phone) will I receive the results of this test?

- Whom should I contact if I don't receive these test results?

## STOPPING A MEDICATION

You experience the world in your own way. You know how you feel. So, it may be difficult to keep taking medication(s) if you no longer feel a condition interferes with your daily life. It can be difficult if you don't like the way a medication makes your body feel. If you think you need to stop taking your medicine, consult with a **licensed medical practitioner** (such as a doctor or a licensed nurse practitioner). Talk with this provider about the pros and cons of stopping a medication. You may actually need to change to something that works better for you. Stopping medication on your own can hurt you physically and emotionally. It can harm those around you, including your family and friends. If you need to stop taking a medication, your doctor or nurse practitioner needs to help you plan how to do that safely.

**YOU ARE HERE:**

## Guiding Star Point Four Review

**1.** The facts in your files tell a story about you. As an independent adult with your own voice, managing your own information means taking charge of your story.

**2.** Your job as information manager has five parts: (1) *organize* records, (2) *maintain* the treatment plan routine, (3) *record* treatment progress and other observations in daily life, (4) *share* this information with your providers, and (5) *inquire* about any health information that can help you understand your own care.

**3.** A two-inch, three-ring binder is a good way to keep paperwork organized and available for appointments, phone calls, and anytime you need to check information.

**4.** Pharmacists can be excellent sources of information about medications. Most are willing to spend time making sure you have all the facts. Pharmacists also know a lot about your prescription drug insurance.

**5.** A solid routine is the key to taking medications safely. Put your medications in a seven-day pill organizer (if you are not required to keep them in the original containers). Consider using reminder apps or **Activity 4.2, My Medication Log**.

**6.** Make written notes in a journal (or use the Activity worksheets with this Guide) to make notes about side effects and other incidents that happen between visits. It can be hard to remember past details during an appointment. Share what's happening honestly with your provider.

**7.** Ask questions about your medications, tests, and any information in your files you don't understand. This is YOUR story, and the information affects decisions about YOUR life.

Change the conversation

YOU
ARE
HERE

GUIDING STAR
POINT FIVE

# Find Support

Create a network of people and resources
that can help you stay safe and cope with
challenges along your journey.

*Learning to navigate virtual, online, and "In Real Life" communities is important for two reasons. First, you can stay safe. Second, you can start creating a "personal network" of people and resources that will uplift your spirit and help you stay strong.*

## Why Find Support?

Everybody needs support!

**Navigating systems** (organizations and agencies that provide services) can help you solve many problems. Still, life gets complicated! Some problems show up again. Solutions may not work out. That's why independent adults in our society must also navigate **communities** to meet their needs. Communities are groups of people who gather together for a shared purpose. A college neighborhood and an online support group are types of communities.

A typical young adult spends many hours each day connecting with others by text, email, or social media. Millions of people participate in **RPGs** and **MMORPGs** (role-playing games and massive multi-player online role-playing games). New forms of media keep changing the way people communicate with one another. Popular apps bring people with shared interests into the same physical meeting space. Some of these opportunities are wonderful and helpful, especially if you feel isolated. Some can create more issues, or even dangers.

### Building Your Personal Network

Learning to navigate these virtual, online, and "In Real Life" communities is important for two reasons. First, you can stay safe. Second, you can start creating a "personal network" of people and resources that will uplift your spirit and help you stay strong. Gaining independence may be very important to you right now. However, **staying** independent means knowing you can meet challenges. Whether it's a lost wallet, a broken relationship, a serious **trauma**, or a really bad day at work, your personal support network is the glue that holds a life together.

Your **role** in finding support is to:

1. Know how to locate resources that might help you in a challenging situation or emergency.

2. Be aware of your own emotional health, so you know when to seek support.

3. Identify a group of trusted people who can offer reliable advice and help.

4. Think critically (judge for yourself, with the help of trusted people) about information, images, and offers that reach you online or through social media. Share information safely.

5. Explore activities that bring you into contact with people who share your interests and support your strengths.

# Part One:
# LOCATE RESOURCES TO MEET CHALLENGES

Locating resources means creating a list of where to go, what to do, and whom to contact if things don't happen the way you expected. Sometimes it can be hard to think clearly in a challenging situation. You might feel rushed or panicked. When you have the first few steps of a back-up plan, you can take a deep breath. Once you start living out your plan, other solutions will be easier to find.

What types of resources do you need in your back-up plan? Start by looking at your own strengths and concerns. You can use the worksheets in Guiding Star Point One (Set Goals): Activity 1.1, "What Are My Strengths?" and Activity 1.2, "What Are My Concerns?" This allows you to look down the road and see where issues might occur.

> \* See Activity 1.1, What Are My Strengths?

> \* See Activity 1.2, What Are My Concerns?"

For example, let's say one of the strengths you listed was an apartment close to a bus line that you can take to your job. A concern you listed was "I'm worried about covering my bills." If you can't pay for a monthly bus pass, you won't get to work. You might even get stranded somewhere late at night. Here's how your strategy might work:

- Your first solution might be to look for resources that can lower the cost of transportation (such as a student or disability discount).

- You talk to your case manager. She helps you find an insurance program that will **reimburse** you (pay you back after you have spent money) for some transportation expenses. This means you can use a taxi (such as Uber or Lyft, if you have a debit card) when a bus isn't available. The case manager advises saving a little extra money if you want to use this program, because it takes a few weeks to get a reimbursement check.

- You and your case manager work on a budget. You find that after your bus pass expenses, you can put aside $15 for a "taxi" fund. That money will get reimbursed every month, so the fund will grow. The paperwork for that program seems complicated, so you ask for help.

- Meanwhile, the mental health agency has some one-time bus passes for clients, so the case manager gives you one to keep in case of emergency. Now you have a plan (use resources that lower costs), a back-up plan (use money you have saved to take a taxi when you need one, because you can get reimbursed later), and a possible emergency plan (use a free, one-time bus pass).

> \* See Activity 5.1, Building a Back Up Plan

## RESOURCES FOR FOOD AND HOUSING

If you have concerns that might affect your health and safety, look for resources before the issue becomes a crisis. You may be concerned about **unstable housing** (you have a place to live or stay now, but it isn't safe, or you may have to leave soon). Another example is **low food security** (you don't often eat nourishing food because you—or the people with whom you live—can't afford it). Start with agencies where you already receive services, such as a **community mental health agency** or **system of care**. Talk to your case manager. Be honest about your situation. You can also call 211 or go to http://211.org to find out about services available in your local community.

## WALK BESIDE ME

**Companioning** is a term that describes how a family member or friend can "walk beside you" to give advice and support or help you make decisions. The family member or friend doesn't take over or make the decisions for you. That person might show you how to do a task or might explain a task and watch as you do it. (For example, the person might say, "When you call the Medicaid helpline, here are three things to say. I'll stand right here and listen.") As you make choices, he or she might say, "How did that work for you?" or "Have you thought of this?" However, you choose to have that person involved, you take the actions, and you make the final decisions.

Building this type of relationship isn't always easy, especially if that person is a parent or other family member who had authority over you as a child. This is a big adjustment in your lives! It takes patience. It takes a willingness to speak honestly, listen to the other's point of view, and start over when things aren't working.

## Part Two: BE AWARE OF YOUR EMOTIONS AND BEHAVIOR

Six Questions to Determine if You Need Additional Support:

1. **What are you feeling right now and why?**
   Write down what you are feeling and possible causes for those feelings.

2. **Are you feeling safe right now?**
   Why or why not?

3. **If you are not feeling safe, whom can you contact?** Examples might include family members, friends, case manager, therapist, or crisis hotlines.

   Follow the directions provided by your support network. This might include getting an appointment to see your service provider earlier than planned, having your medication adjusted, or (if necessary) getting temporary inpatient treatment.

4. **After speaking with your support network, how do you feel?**
   If you feel fine, that's great! Continue to follow your plan.
   If you do not feel safe, continue through the rest of the questions.

5. **If you cannot contact your support network, what is the next step?**
   This might include calling a crisis hotline or going to your local mental health center to be assessed for further treatment.

6. **If you still don't feel safe, what is your next move?**
   You may need to go directly to your local mental health center (which may be called a **Community Mental Health Agency**) for **assessment**. If that's not possible and you need immediate help, you may need to call **Mobile Crisis** or 911.

## Part Three: BUILD YOUR NETWORK OF TRUST

Your goal as an independent adult is to use your own voice and make as many of your own decisions as possible. However, we are really "interdependent," because we all need help from one another sometimes. (In fact, some transition programs for young adults now feature "interdependent living" options. For example, a less experienced young adult might share an apartment with a more experienced roommate who can teach basic skills. (This is someone with whom the young adult is not romantically involved.)

Here are some ways that trusted people in your life might handle decisions about finances (money and bills) or health care.

A **Durable Power of Attorney (POA)** is a legal process for giving a trusted friend or relative the right to handle certain responsibilities for you when you are not physically or mentally able to do so. For example, this trusted friend or relative may pay bills or make medical decisions for you in the event of a serious accident or **mental incapacity**.

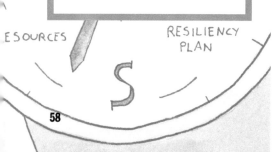

STREN

ESOURCES

RESILIENCY PLAN

The two types of documents needed are the **Medical (Healthcare) Power of Attorney** and the **Financial Power of Attorney**. It's important to know that a POA does not give away your power to make decisions. It only takes effect during the time that you are unable to make decisions. You may also revoke (take back) a POA at any time by filing another legal document.

You may give POA to another person without going to court. To find the forms you need, search on the words "power of attorney" to find free and low-cost **legal templates** (fill in forms). Be sure to choose the template for the state where you live and follow all of the instructions. You don't need a lawyer to get any of these documents.

**Guardianship** (called **conservatorship** in some states) is a state court proceeding in which a person is given the legal right to make decisions for someone else. A **guardian** or **conservator** can be appointed to make decisions for a person who is under age 18 or is unable to make decisions because of a permanent disability. During this legal process, the court appoints a lawyer to act as **guardian ad litem** (advocate for the child or person with a disability) to gather information about the person's choices. If a person is disabled, the court tries to make sure the person agrees to give up his or her rights to make legal decisions. The person may be asked to choose who they want the court to appoint as guardian or conservator. Ordinarily, a person who has a guardian or conservator cannot legally sign a contract (or use a credit card). The guardian/conservator must handle all financial and other legal decisions, including where that person will live. Arranging a guardianship or conservatorship can cost between $500-$2000, depending on where you live and the details of the case.

## "I" STATEMENTS THAT LEAD TO ANSWERS

Mental Health America offers a short set of "I" statements (such as "I think I'm showing symptoms") to help you decide whether and how to get help. Each statement is linked to a source of information or support. Go to http://mentalhealthamerica.net/im-looking-mental-health-help-myself.

## ONLINE EMOTIONAL SUPPORT

Online support groups can be sources of great comfort to people who feel isolated. The website http://wikihow.com suggests that one way to determine if a "chat board" or online group is right for you is by reading through a long thread of posts. Do members offer each other compassion and understanding? Do they seem knowledgeable? Do they quote sources? How do they handle disagreement? Is there a moderator? Are guidelines posted to let people know what kind of behavior is acceptable? "Examine the dates and frequency of posts and discussions to verify that the community is active. A strong online support community will contain updated news and information about your issue," adds wikihow.

## Part Four: THINK CRITICALLY ABOUT SOCIAL MEDIA

Protecting your online space is like locking your front door, except that it's much harder to do, because new scams (illegal attempts to trick others into giving money) and other online threats appear so often. Good rules of thumb:

- Don't open attachments in emails from people you don't know. Don't open attachments in emails from people you *do* know if the email address or the message seems odd to you. The account may have been hacked. Opening the attachment will spread the virus/worm (also called malware) to your account.

- Be extremely cautious about giving out any personal details on social media sites. Never give out your full address. Check the security and privacy of your personal information on social media by checking the privacy settings for your account(s).

- Don't forward bullying content or messages. Report incidents to moderators, website administrators, and "safety centers" that exist on big sites such as YouTube or Facebook.

- Use credit or debit cards on secure websites only. The "checkout" portion of these websites will typically show a well-known shopping cart (for example, PayPal or Shopify) or will mention a security measure called an "SSL certificate."

- Be aware that purchasing and/or sending some forms of pornography over the internet is illegal, particularly if the material involves underaged persons or illegal acts. You could go to jail and also damage your reputation.

## Explaining Social Media

It may feel very frustrating if others (such as parents and older mentors) don't understand the online social media, apps, or games you enjoy. They may not understand the relationships you form with people you meet online or what these activities mean to you. A good strategy is to lead with the facts. Try to explain how social media, games, and apps work (or get parents/mentors involved, if appropriate). Use your internet research skills to find persuasive articles or other evidence that support your point of view. Be as patient as possible. Use "I" statements, such as "I like this game because...." or "I feel good about myself when I use this app because...." However, stay open to the possibility that parents, mentors, or friends may have good instincts about a situation. People who care about you may see changes in your health or personality that you don't notice yourself. Keep the conversation going.

# Part Five: CONSIDER COMMUNITY

A strong personal network includes **natural supports**. This term means friends, family, neighbors, or others in the community who provide help without being part of a paid service. Who helps you right now? Try making a list of people who touch your life right now. Try to list at least one thing you could count on each person to do if you needed it. A strong personal network can grow when no one person is asked to do too much.

Also think about what you like to do. Consider broadening your personal network by trying to get involved in at least one new community that relates to one of your interests. Look for events that interest you. Explore a support group, youth council meeting, or drop-in center. Volunteer for one activity. Don't rush it. Developing natural supports can take time for some people. However, keep in mind that donating time to help others can make you healthier and can make your personal network stronger.

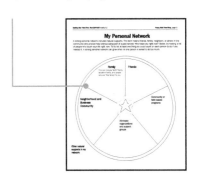

✳ **See Activity 5.2, My Personal Network**

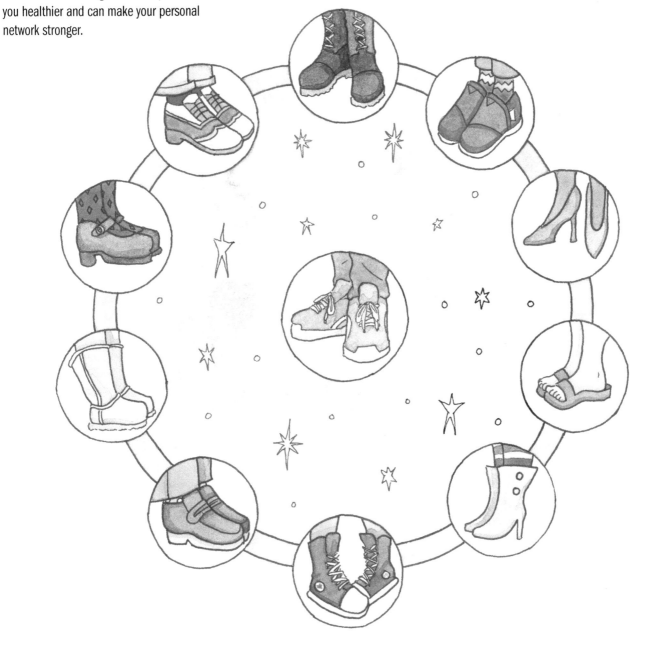

## MENTAL HEALTH SUPPORT

For rock-solid information about mental illness in teens and young adults, try Mental Health America's "Life on Campus" website http://mentalhealthamerica.net/life-campus and the Teens/Young Adult pages of the National Alliance on Mental Illness (NAMI) website http://nami.org/Find-Support/Teens-and-Young-Adults. The Mental Health America (MHA) site offers dozens of short, useful articles and aids for college students (include step-by-step deep breathing exercises and a printable coloring book for lowering stress). MHA also offers online support groups. NAMI's http://ok2talk.org/ tumblr blog offers young adults a safe, moderated place to post thoughts, feelings, and expressions.

## Living An Independent and Interdependent Life

One very important task for any young adult is learning to live an independent life in which you can make choices and use your own voice. The other very important task is learning to live an "interdependent" life. In that life, your strengths are nourished. You cherish and are cherished by a community of friends and family (biological or not) who care about what happens to you. You have a purpose and a place in the world.

## YOU ARE HERE:

# Guiding Star Point Five Review

1. Create a back-up plan for where to go and what to do in a challenging situation or emergency. Look at your own strengths and concerns to determine where you might need more resources. Start with the agencies where you now get services, as they may have programs to help you. If you are concerned about having stable housing or enough food, don't wait until these issues result in a crisis.

2. Take time to stay in touch with what you are feeling, so you know when to seek support.

3. Identify a person (or more than one person) you can trust to act for you in an emergency. You can give a family member or friend a **Medical (Healthcare) Power of Attorney** and **Financial Power of Attorney,** so they can make medical decisions or pay your bills if you are seriously ill or injured. (You do not have to give both these documents to the same person.)

4. Be cautious about how you share personal details on social media. Never give out your full address. Check your security and privacy settings on social media accounts. Read through past threads on "chat boards" or online support groups to see if members seem knowledgeable about issues and show compassion toward each other.

5. Consider getting involved in a new community that relates to one of your interests. Attend an event, support group, youth council meeting, or drop-in center. Volunteer to help. Contributing to a community can raise your spirits and make your personal network stronger.

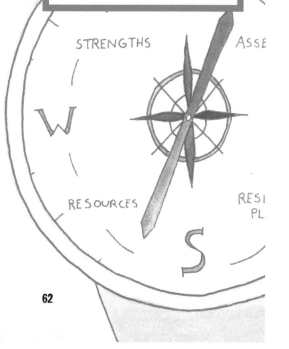

YOU
ARE
HERE

YOUR FUTURE
NEXT 5 EXITS ↗

GUIDING STAR CLOSE-UP:

# The Bridge to Everywhere

Use a five-point plan to navigate transition services.

## Why Plan Transition Services?

Your "Transition Job Description" is to learn strategies and take actions that lead to the everyday life you want—right now, a year or two down the road, and later in your future. The *Guiding Star* provides an organized, step-by-step way to move through this journey at your own pace. For example, you may set a goal to live in your own apartment, but right now you feel comfortable staying with your family. (Guiding Star Point One). You might begin learning how your mental health system works or how to communicate effectively with doctors, while someone you trust still goes with you to appointments. (Guiding Star Points Two and Three). It's OK. The timeline is up to you.

However, there are "bridges" between **systems** that young adults must cross within a certain period of time to get the services they need. For example, if you choose to go to college right after graduating from high school, you need to meet application deadlines. New stages of life can be exciting, but the details can sometimes feel overwhelming too. Luckily, all five points of the *Guiding Star* can help you cross those bridges. When you feel pressured to make choices, you can *change the conversation* with others (and that worried voice inside your head!) to focus on practical next steps.

Young adults between the ages of 18 and 22 must cross certain bridges if they receive state or federal government services. These include:

### Special Education: Life After High School

A person who receives **special education** services may stay in high school until the end of the year in which he/she turns 22, even if that person has enough credits to receive a high school diploma. By law, starting at age 14 and no later than age 16, a student must have a **Transition Plan** that describes that person's intended path for areas of life, such as housing, transportation, health, daily needs, and involvement in community.

**Questions to consider/discuss with others:**

1. When should I leave high school? (At age 18, or wait until later, so I have more time to develop practical or social skills and experience?)

2. Should I start an education, training, or work program right after high school? What is available? How do I qualify? When do I need to apply?

3. What skills do I need to learn in my high school program that will help me live as independently as possible? Do the Transition Plan goals in my IEP need to be changed to include more practical goals and different services? How do we do that?

**Ways you might use the five points of the *Guiding Star*:**

**Set Goals:** Review the Transition Plan in your **IEP**. Consider: *Does it still reflect what I think I want for my everyday life? Identify my top three concerns about leaving high school at* *age 18. Identify my top three concerns about staying in high school a few more years. If you don't/didn't have an IEP in high school, it is still important to think about what you want for your everyday life and what your top concerns may be.*

**Learn System Basics:** Find ways to gather information about transition planning that fit your learning style. Look for online and print sources about your rights to services under the **IDEA 2004.** Start with your state's Department of Education website. Consider: *What are the most important questions I need answered right now?*

**Build Relationships:** Make a list of questions to bring to the IEP meeting or meeting with your **case manager.** Talk to a trusted person ahead of time. Consider: *For the IEP meeting, what is my* **role**? *Who can help me learn how to do my part? Does the team seem to understand my goals?*

**Manage Information:** Make a binder to keep records, including your personal copies of all IEP documents and documents for/from other meetings. Consider: *What records do I need to apply for services? Do I need to get any tests or assessments to qualify for services? Do I understand the data in my records?*

**Find Support:** Look for peer support. Consider: *Where can my family and I find others who have been through the process of seeking services? Can the school or a* **family advocacy organization** *put us in touch with other families who have had similar experiences? What online resources can help me make decisions?*

## Health/Mental Health/Insurance: New Providers

Children who are covered by Medicaid (which may be called by another name in your state) may be switched to a new network of providers at age 18. Depending on the government programs where you live, you may notice no difference at all and just get a new health insurance card in the mail. In other cases, you may have a certain amount of time to choose a provider (called an **enrollment period**). Otherwise, you may be assigned to a provider group. (That may be OK, or it may give you a provider you don't prefer.) Some types of coverage you received as a child (for example, vision and dental services) may not be part of your adult plan at all.

### Questions to consider/discuss with others:

1. Will I be switched to a new community health/mental health center for my services? Do I have to choose (enroll in) a new plan by a certain date? When? How do I do that? What are my choices?

2. Will I have vision (eye-check-ups and glasses) and dental care as part of my new coverage? If not, how will I pay for vision and dental services? (If not age 18 yet, what can I do to get my needs met while I still have coverage?)

## THE AGE 26 INSURANCE BRIDGE

Young adults can be covered under their families' private health insurance plans until they turn 26. It's very important to start researching plans several months ahead so all paperwork gets done by your 26th birthday and there is no gap in insurance coverage. If you are eligible for health insurance through an employer, that tends to be the best. However, make sure the coverage is affordable given your current needs. (For example, if you take expensive medications that are not covered by your prescription drug benefit, you will have to pay **out-of-pocket** or find other programs to cover your costs.) If you have a disability or very low income, call your local Medicaid office or visit the state government website for information about public health insurance options. Visit https://www.healthcare.gov to learn about **subsidized** plans. Visit http://211.org or call 211 to search for community organizations that help people locate the best insurance plans and fill out forms. (See Guiding Star Point Two for more information about insurance plans.)

*New stages of life can be exciting, but the details can sometimes feel overwhelming too. Luckily, all five points of the Guiding Star can help you cross those bridges.*

**Ways to use the five points of the *Guiding Star*:**

**Set Goals:** List your top three concerns about switching to a new insurance plan or getting insurance from a different insurance provider.

**Learn System Basics:** If you have Medicaid, go to your member website address on the back of insurance ID card and look for information about what happens when you turn 18. You can also call the number on your card.

**Build Relationships:** Talk to your case manager. Ask "What are my options?"

**Manage Information:** Find out what records you will need to apply for insurance. Create a binder to keep your records in a single place.

**Find Support:** Look for community resources, such as faith-based organizations and advocacy groups, that help people fill out insurance application forms. Look for resources for getting eyeglasses and dental services.

## Income (Paying for Housing, Food, Transportation, etc.)

Families with limited income, who have children under age 18 with disabilities, can receive Supplemental Security Income (SSI), a monthly government payment. At age 18, a young adult must apply for his or her own payment. (In most cases, the young adult must apply after age 18 and wait for a few months for SSI payments to start. That person eventually gets an extra payment to make up for the gap.)

If you did not receive SSI as a child, you can still apply as a young adult. Your records must show that you had a disability before age 18. You will usually need to get another assessment or letter from a physician to show you still have the disability.

Even if you and your family don't need the money, qualifying for SSI can sometimes be a "gateway" to being accepted into other state government programs, such as Medicaid, vocational rehabilitation (a program to assist you in finding work or training to work), or transportation supports. Sometimes it means you go to the head of the line for programs with long waiting lists.

A young adult over age 18 with a disability may still qualify for SSI, even if he or she still lives at home. (This is called being a "Household of One," even though you don't physically live in your own household.) When you live on your own (paying your own rent and at least half of your own expenses), your SSI payment is increased.

**Questions to consider/discuss with others:**

1. Am I still eligible for SSI based on my disability? What do I need to do? What documents do I need? When should I start the process of qualifying for SSI?

2. How soon after I apply will I know if I am accepted? If I am accepted, when will payments start?

3. How does my SSI payment change if I move to my own place? Will the payment provide enough money to meet my bills every month? If not, does qualifying for SSI make it easier to become eligible for other assistance, such as a voucher to reduce the cost of housing or insurance?

**Ways to Use the five points of the *Guiding Star:***

**Set Goals:** Identify a priority, such as making sure you meet deadlines for getting assessments and doing paperwork, so you can start receiving payments a few months after your 18th birthday.

**Learn Systems Basics:** Go to https://www.ssa.gov to set up an appointment with a Social Security case manager to find out what you need to do.

**Build Relationships:** Come to your appointment with the Social Security case manager on time, with a written list of questions. Try to bring a family member or trusted friend with you.

**Manage Information:** Begin collecting the records you will need to submit. Create a binder.

**Find Support:** If there will be a gap in your income or your family's income while you wait for the new SSI paperwork to be processed, look for other resources that can help with your bills.

# Five Resources for Employment and Vocational Services

1. Your state's office of **vocational rehabilitation** services connects people with job training and work opportunities. https://www.careeronestop.org/ResourcesFor/WorkersWith Disabilities/workers-with-disabilities.aspx

2. If you receive SSI, you can still get a job and earn income under the "Ticket to Work" program. (https://choosework.ssa.gov/)

3. Work with an employment development coach.

4. Go to the nearest office of a state employment center. https://careeronestop.org/LocalHelp/service-locator.aspx

5. If possible, you may want to start with volunteer work: https://volunteermatch.org

## LEAVING FOSTER CARE

Young adults who "age out" of the child welfare system go through a transition to independent living between ages 18-22, depending on the programs in their state. Aging out of the child welfare system is an important and complex topic covered outside of *Young Adult Road Map*. One place to look for resources is the federal government website "Child Welfare Information Gateway," https://www.childwelfare.gov/topics/outofhome/independent/resources/. This website offers resources for transition planning, applying for educational financial aid, and working on many other concerns.

## Using Strengths and Concerns in Transition

What strengths can you bring to this problem? What concerns do you have? What are your priorities (services or supports you may need to meet your concerns right now)? Here are some examples of how strengths, concerns, and priorities might be part of your plan as you cross bridges into new stages of life.

| BRIDGE | Strengths | Concerns | Priorities |
|---|---|---|---|
| Education | You are willing to plan. You are willing to listen to advice from others, but make your own decisions. You are willing to ask for help when you need it.<br><br>Your high school counselor advised you to sign up for student disability services when you enroll at college. Though you don't think you'll need it, you meet the disability services office staff and fill out paperwork to be eligible for services. | Three weeks into your first semester, you are struggling in one course and doing okay in other courses. Also, you think the professor who teaches the course you are struggling in doesn't like you. | Reach out to your contact in the disability services office to go over services that are available to you, including class note takers, tutors, quieter testing spaces, longer testing time, and advice on how to communicate effectively with professors. |
| | You are willing and able to plan. You are willing and able to communicate your goals and concerns to others.<br><br>You have been involved in your IEP transition planning process since the age of 14. | You are concerned that the transition goals you and the IEP team wrote last year no longer fit who you are and what you want to do. | Reassemble the team (you, Mom/Dad, guidance counselor, school psychologist, and others) to revise your plan to fit who you are today.<br><br>Bring in a written list of your concerns and potential solutions. |
| Employment | You are willing and able to ask about jobs that would fit you better. | You have had four different jobs in the past six months. You start with high hopes and leave (on your own) in disappointment. | Go to an office of the state's career center to look for an apprenticeship where you learn while you earn money. Ask about an internship where people are willing to teach and explain things to you at a slower pace. Apply for **vocational rehabilitation** benefits to get job training and placement. |
| Health/Mental Health | You are willing and able to choose your own mental health provider. You are willing and able to rethink your treatment plan and to do research to support a new plan.<br><br>You have been researching treatments for your condition and keeping a side effects log about your current medications. | When your insurance plan switches you to a new network, you choose a nurse practitioner. You are concerned that your current treatment plan relies too much on medication. | You talk to the new provider about your current medications and side effects, showing your medication side effects log. You discuss additional measures, such as **psychotherapy**, meditation, and exercise, which may lower the amount of medication you need to take. (See Activity 4.3, "My Side Effects Log.") |

| BRIDGE | Strengths | Concerns | Priorities |
|---|---|---|---|
| Health/Mental Health | You are willing and able to seek advice about choosing therapists. You are open to seeking therapists who provide services online. | You live in a small town. You are concerned that any therapist you choose will have ties to your family and friends. You are concerned about your **right to privacy**. | Look for online reviews about counseling sites and therapists. Seek advice from your insurance plan provider, the Clinical Social Work Association, the database of therapists and support groups on http://PsychologyToday.com, and other resources. |
| Housing and Transportation | You are willing and able to rethink your living arrangement.<br><br>You know how to talk with your life coach about things that are upsetting to you. | Your third roommate in six months just moved out. You and he had a bad argument. The previous two roommates just left while you were at work. After this big fight, you are concerned that you might be the problem. | Talk with your life coach about setting ground rules with roommates. Talk with your life coach about whether you should/can afford to live alone. |

# The College Bridge

When you visit colleges, consider the "SAFER" checklist compiled by the website BestValueSchools.com.

**Social:** Does the school offer social opportunities that are appropriate for students with your needs?

**Academic:** Does the school provide academic supports (test proctors, assistive technology, training for the professors) that are appropriate for your needs?

**Functioning:** Does the school help with the transition from high school to college and from semester to semester? Does the school provide support during academic breaks? Does the school offer psychological and counseling services? Does the school's strategy for communicating with students fit your communication needs? Does the school have a structured peer-support program?

**Employment:** Does the school (or the surrounding community) offer a range of part-time jobs for students with special needs? Can the school's career center help you connect with internships and employment services during college breaks and after you graduate?

**Residential:** Does the school have a residence hall that meets your needs? (Look at aspects such as lighting, noise, social spaces, and location relative to buildings where classes are held). How are roommates assigned? Will that system work for you? Are there other options?

Adapted from: "20 Best Colleges for Students with Autism 2017-2018," Best Value Schools, https://bestvalueschools.com/rankings/students-with-autism/

## IS COLLEGE THE RIGHT CHOICE?

**Less Effective Reasons to Apply**

My parents/caregivers expect me to attend college.

My friends will be attending four-year colleges.

I don't know what else to do after high school. I don't know where else I would fit.

**More Effective Reasons to Apply**

I want to be a lifelong learner.

I want to explore career options that I have not considered before.

I want to acquire skills for a career.

## The Guiding Star for Anywhere You Travel

This Guide can't tell you every **key word** or describe every bridge you will need to cross. So even though *Young Adult Road Map* contains many practical strategies, it mostly tells **how** to navigate, not **what** those **systems** are all about, nor what the solutions to certain concerns might be. Young adults in this country who receive health and social services have certain things in common, but YOUR path is unique. The fact is that **transition planning** has many parts, and transition programs vary from state to state.

However, the *Guiding Star*, just like the North Star in the sky, doesn't change. Although laws, programs, procedures, and rules change all the time, **people in systems tend to act in very predictable ways**, no matter what services they provide. People in every system use "key words" to exchange information. They build working relationships to get their jobs done. When you know this basic truth, you are empowered to face any unfamiliar situation. The more you use your navigation skills to solve problems, the more confident you will feel. Facing unfamiliar situations with confidence is one of the greatest strengths any person can have on a journey into the future.

### YOU ARE HERE:

## Guiding Star Close-up Review

1. There are certain "bridges" between **systems** that young adults must cross **within a certain time period** to get the services they need. Luckily, all five points of the *Guiding Star* can help you cross those bridges.

2. By law, starting at age 14 and no later than age 16, a student in **special education** must have a **Transition Plan** that describes that person's intended path for different areas of life. You are part of the **IEP** team. Find ways to gather information about transition planning that fit your learning style. Do the goals lead to the everyday life you want to live?

3. If you have Medicaid or other public health insurance, go to the member website address on the back of your insurance ID card or call the number on the card to get information about what happens when you turn 18.

4. If you received **Supplemental Security Income (SSI)** as a child under 18 or think you may qualify for SSI as a disabled low-income adult over 18, go to https://ssa. gov to find more information and set up an appointment with a case manager.

5. An effective way to cut a problem down to size is to begin by making four lists: What strengths can I bring to this problem? What concerns do I have? What are my priorities (most important concerns right now)? What services and supports would help me with those priority concerns?

# Glossary

## A

**Accommodations and modifications.** Changes made in a regular education program to help a youth make educational progress. Certain criteria must be met to be eligible for these changes (see 504 Plan).

**Acute.** Symptoms that are both temporary and severe.

**Adolescent.** A person who is in transition between childhood and adulthood. The World Health Organization defines adolescence as the years between age 10 and 19.

**Advocacy organization/advocacy group.** An organization that is dedicated to helping people navigate systems to get what they need. The group may also work to influence other people and systems to change laws and procedures.

**Affected child.** A child who shows symptoms of a behavioral health or other disorder.

**Agenda.** A document that lists the main points to be covered in an IEP meeting.

**Alternative medicine/complementary and alternative medicine/ CAM.** Alternative medicine includes medical products and practices that are not part of "standard care." Standard care practices are based on the results of scientific research and are widely used by doctors and nurses. Examples of alternative practices include homeopathy (herbal medicine), traditional medicine, chiropractic, and acupuncture. "Complementary medicine" or "complementary and alternative medicine" (CAM) usually means alternatives are being used together with standard treatment. A common example would be using massage or meditation with standard medical treatment. (As such alternatives are used more widely, they may become part of standard care.)

**Annual (IEP) goal.** An educational goal that the school system expects the youth to reach by the end of the school year, as part of his or her Individualized Education Program (IEP).

**Annual IEP review.** A meeting to review a child's or youth's IEP and make any necessary changes in goals, services, or placement in the next school year.

**Annual or lifetime maximum benefit.** The maximum amount a patient will be required to pay per year for certain types of treatment under the terms of your health insurance plan.

**Annual out-of-pocket maximum.** The maximum amount a patient will be required to pay for certain types of treatment under the terms of your health insurance plan.

**Appeal.** A formal request for a decision to be changed by a higher authority.

**Areas of need.** Broad categories in which a youth needs to improve in order to make progress in school, as determined by the IEP team and included in the IEP document.

**Assessment.** The evaluation of a person's medical, behavioral, or education condition in order to determine what services the person needs.

**Assessment team.** A team of school staff or consultants assigned by the school to evaluate a youth. For behavioral health issues, the team usually includes a psychologist and may include specialists in certain disorders.

**At-risk.** In possible danger, especially for developing a problem.

**Attention Deficit Hyperactivity Disorder (ADHD)/Attention Deficit Disorder (ADD).** A chronic (long-lasting or happening again and again) condition that makes it difficult for a person to organize, stay focused, make realistic plans, or think before acting. People with ADHD may show more symptoms related to moving around or not being able to sit still easily (hyperactivity) than people with ADD.

**Authorize, authorization, pre-authorization, prior authorization.** Approval given by the insurance company for a treatment that is shown to be medically necessary and covered by the person's health care benefits.

**Authorized representative.** Someone who is legally assigned to speak, act, or receive information on behalf of another person.

## B

**Behavior.** A person's actions, speech, or manner of expressing themselves.

# Glossary

**Behavioral health (also called mental health).** A person's mental well-being, which includes thoughts, feelings, emotions, and behavior.

**Behavioral health organization (BHO).** An insurance company that manages benefit plans for mental (behavioral) health or substance (drug and alcohol) abuse treatment.

**Behavioral health specialist.** A trained and licensed/certified provider who can assess, evaluate, and treat persons with behavioral health issues.

**Benefits (also called coverage).** The contract between an insurance company and the insured person, promising to pay for certain treatments under certain conditions.

**Black-box warning.** A Food and Drug Administration (FDA) warning that alerts doctors to a possibly serious side effect or complication that might be caused by giving a medication under certain conditions.

# C

**Cap.** The limit on the amount of money that a health insurance policy/plan will pay for certain services.

**Care manager.** A type of case manager for a health insurance plan whose job it is to help people find options for getting treatment approved or to solve unusual problems with the benefits plan.

**Case manager.** A staff member in a medical, behavioral health, education, or insurance setting whose job is to set up services, coordinate services, and/or help solve problems for a client.

**Certified.** Eligible (allowed) to receive special education services. A youth has to be certified under one of the IDEA 2004 law's 13 disability categories in order to receive special education services.

**Chronic.** A condition or situation, which is long-lasting or occurs again and again.

**Claim (insurance).** A request to get a certain service or treatment paid by the insurance company.

**Clinical assessment report (also called clinical evaluation report).** The written report that follows a clinical assessment/evaluation. This report may include the reason for a person's evaluation, summary of the person's health history, test results and explanations, and recommendations for treatment.

**Clinical diagnosis.** A health provider's description of a problem; made after an evaluation (sometimes called an assessment) is performed.

**Clinician (also called clinical provider).** A provider (usually a clinical psychologist or licensed clinical social worker) who evaluates a client; may also provide therapy.

**Communities.** Groups of people that gather together for a specific purpose. Examples include a college neighborhood, online support groups, political groups, religious groups, etc.

**Community Mental Health Agency (CMHA).** A large mental health center that has a contract to provide services to people who are enrolled in public health insurance plans; sometimes called a Community Mental Health Organization (CMHO) or a Community Mental Health Center (CMHC).

**Community resources.** Agencies, organizations, and programs that provide services for people with different types of needs.

**Comorbid diagnosis.** An additional or "secondary" diagnosis, when a person shows symptoms for more than one disorder.

**Companioning.** A term that describes how a family member or friend can provide support by listening, watching, and making suggestions as a young adult begins to navigate systems

**Complaint.** A written statement that describes a problem a person is having with a provider or service. The complaint should include names, dates, times, and other factual information related to the issue.

**Comprehensive assessment.** See "School evaluation."

**Comprehensive psychiatric treatment.** Mental/behavioral health treatment in a campus-like setting for those who require it on a long-term basis.

**Confidential.** Information about a patient that a health provider cannot tell police, employers, or others not involved in the person's treatment, except under certain conditions (for example, if a crime may be or has been committed).

**Consent.** Legal permission a person gives to others to take an action or release personal information.

**Continuum of care.** The care options available for behavioral health patients, ranging from a short office visit to inpatient hospital treatment.

**Co-payment or co-pay.** An amount you must pay when you visit a healthcare provider. Varies according to health plan.

**Coverage (also called benefits).** The contract between an insurance company and the insured person, promising to pay for certain treatments under certain conditions.

**Crisis intervention.** Psychiatric assistance during a period of extreme distress.

**Criteria (one criterion, many criteria).** Standards that must be met to qualify to receive certain services.

**Cumulative Record (CR).** A youth's permanent school record.

**Customer services (or member services) representative.** An insurance company employee who answers routine questions or solves problems by phone.

# D

**Day treatment program.** This intensive treatment program provides psychiatric treatment with special education for school age youth, and may provide treatment with other programming for young adults.

**Deductible.** The amount of money a person must pay out-of-pocket before the person's insurance plan will begin to pay for certain types of services.

**Denied.** Not approved for paid coverage of services under a particular health plan.

**Development.** The process of growth or advancement (for example, from one stage of life to another).

**Diagnosis.** The broad term health providers use to describe a problem. A behavioral health diagnosis is reached after an evaluation, which may include conversations with you and others, as well as tests, examinations, and/or laboratory studies.

**Diagnostic and Statistical Manual of Mental Disorders (DSM).** A publication of the American Psychiatric Association that lists and describes behavioral health disorders. Healthcare providers use the DSM categories to diagnose illnesses.

**Disability, disabling condition, or 13 disability categories.** A condition that interferes with a youth's ability to learn or function at the same level as others of the same age.

**Disorders.** Conditions in which physical changes, thoughts, feelings, or behaviors cause problems with activities and daily living.

**Drug interactions.** Possible problems that may occur when one drug is used at the same time as another drug.

**Drug screening examination.** A medical test (usually by blood, urine, or hair sample) that tests for illegal substances within the body.

**Due process rights.** Procedures that must be followed to appeal a decision made by an organization, such as a school system or a mental health center.

**Durable power of attorney.** A legal process for assigning a trusted family member or friend to make decisions for a person if he or she becomes physically or mentally unable to do so. For example, this trusted friend or relative might pay bills or make medical decisions for you in the event of a serious accident.

# E

**Early and Periodic Screening, Diagnosis, and Treatment program (EPSDT).** A public health insurance program aimed at finding, diagnosing, and treating problems in children and youth.

**Electronic medical records.** Medical records that are stored and filed in a computer system.

**Eligible.** Qualified to receive treatment or services, because certain conditions have been met. For example, you can be eligible for a program because of your age, disability, or income level.

**Eligibility meeting.** A meeting to determine whether a youth is eligible to receive special education services. This meeting always includes the parent of a youth under 18, if he or she is willing and able to be involved.

# Glossary

**Eligibility report.** A report that determines whether or not a youth is qualified to receive special education services because a regular education program cannot meet educational needs.

**Emerging adulthood (also called transition to adulthood).** The period between age 14 to 26 (up to age 30 according to some opinions), in which a person is in the process of becoming an adult.

**Enrollment period.** The amount of time some insurance programs allow for choosing (enrolling in) a plan or provider network.

**Evaluate/evaluation.** The process of examining a person's condition or behavior to find out more about the problem. An evaluation can include conversations with you and others, a physical examination, other tests, and laboratory studies.

**Evidence.** A set of facts that can be observed and measured.

**Exclusions.** Types of treatment that an insurance plan will not pay for under certain conditions.

**Expected progress.** How much educational or developmental progress the state expects a youth of a certain age to make under typical circumstances.

**Extended School Year program (ESY).** An IEP developed for the summer months to help a youth keep up with the progress he or she has made during the school year.

# F

**Facilitator.** A person who runs or directs a meeting.

**Family advocacy organization.** An organization that provides information, training, or support to families and works to influence the public, legislators, or government agencies. (See also Advocacy Organizations/Advocacy Groups).

**Family Education Rights and Privacy Act (FERPA).** A federal law regulating how a youth's school records can be used.

**Family medicine practitioner.** Sometimes known as a primary care provider, family doctor, family practice doctor, or primary care practitioner; a provider who sees patients for general healthcare needs.

**Federally Qualified Healthcare Center.** A local healthcare center that can assess and treat patients.

**Field care managers.** Special case managers employed by a Managed Care Organization or Behavioral Health Organization that is based in the local community.

**Financial Power of Attorney.** A legal process in which a trusted family member or friend makes financial decisions or pays bills if a person becomes physically or mentally unable to do so. A financial power of attorney document is one form of Durable Power of Attorney (See also Medical/Health Care Power of Attorney).

**504 Plan.** An educational plan that lists accommodations and modifications that will help a student who meets certain criteria make progress in a regular education program. Some youth with behavioral health disorders who do not qualify for special education services under the IDEA 2004 law can qualify for 504 Plan accommodations.

**Flexible benefits.** A commitment from the insurance company that money targeted to pay for one type of health plan benefit (for example, in-patient hospital treatment) can be used for another level of care (such as residential treatment).

**Free Application for Federal Student Aid (FAFSA).** A form that can be prepared annually by current and prospective college students (undergraduate and graduate) in the United States to determine their eligibility for student financial aid.

**Free Appropriate Public Education (FAPE).** A youth's right, under the federal IDEA 2004 law, to an education "designed to meet his or her unique needs." Guarantees the right to special education services when the regular education program cannot meet the youth's needs because of a disability.

# G

**Gender non-conforming.** A person whose behavior and appearance do not match society's expectations of someone of that gender.

**Gender orientation.** A person's internal sense of whether they are male or female, a combination of both, or neither.

**Genetic predisposition.** A tendency to develop an illness that is inherited through one or both biological parents. A predisposition means a person may possibly develop that illness, and so should be watched carefully for symptoms.

**Genetic traits.** Physical qualities, mental qualities, or conditions a person inherits from a biological ("blood") relative.

**Good-faith effort.** A legal term that means the person or agency has shown a sincere effort to be fair, honest, and willing to solve problems.

**Grievance.** A formal, written complaint to a higher authority about a problem with a provider or service.

**Guardian/guardianship (conservator/conservatorship).** A state court proceeding in which a person is given the legal right to make decisions for someone else.

**Guardian ad litem.** A person, appointed by a court, who serves as an advocate for a child or youth, or a person with a disability, during a guardianship proceeding.

**Guidelines (insurance).** Rules set up to determine the conditions under which certain treatment services will be approved for payment by an insurance plan.

# H

**Health history or health history form.** A form that contains basic information about a person's medical history. This will usually include physical diseases, behavioral health issues, medications, allergies, immunizations, family health history, and developmental history.

**Health insurance policy/plan.** A contract to pay certain health care costs. The plan states what the company and the individual will pay (for example, premiums, caps, deductibles, co-pays, out-of-pocket maximums, etc.).

**Health Insurance Portability and Accountability Act (HIPPA).** Federal law requiring health care providers, under certain conditions, to get permission before releasing patient information.

# I

**IEP document.** A legal agreement (Individualized Education Program), signed by the school system representative, parent(s) or guardians, and youth (if he or she is over 16) that describes goals, services, and placement to be provided for a youth with a disability.

**Impact on educational performance.** See "educational impact."

**Individualized Education Program (IEP).** A program of educational services for a student with a disability. In the school system, this term is often used to refer to 1) a meeting to certify a youth for special education services; 2) the education plan written at this meeting; and 3) the legal document that describes the program.

**Individualized Family Service Plan.** A plan developed by a social agency to provide services to a youth or family.

**Individuals with Disabilities Education Improvement Act of 2004 (IDEA 2004).** A federal law that guarantees the right to educational services for students with disabilities aged three through 21 (or through the end of the school year in which an eligible student turns 22).

**In-network providers.** A member of a group of health care providers who can provide treatment to a patient under the terms of a health insurance plan.

**Inpatient psychiatric unit.** A special unit in a hospital where patients with severe behavioral health problems stay 24 hours per day while receiving treatment.

**Insurance policy/plan.** See "Health insurance policy/plan."

**Intake interview.** The first appointment with a new health provider or social agency. At an intake interview, the client or patient gives information and discusses symptoms or concerns.

**Integrated care.** A treatment approach in which providers work together to give the best care for a patient.

# K

**Key words.** Important words used by systems and organizations to exchange important information and decide whether someone is eligible to get services.

# L

**Legal templates.** Free or low-cost legal documents that have fillable blanks for people to use. Can usually be found online or by asking a provider.

# Glossary

**Lesbian, Gay, Bisexual, Queer/Questioning, Intersex, and 2-Spirited (LGBTQI2-S).** Sexual identifications for people who do not identify as heterosexual.

**Licensed medical practitioner.** A provider who is licensed/certified by the state to practice medicine.

**Local Education Agency (LEA) representative.** The school official at an IEP meeting who has the power to make the final agreement between a youth, the parent or guardian of a youth, and the school system about the youth's educational program.

**Low Food Security.** Lack of access to enough nutritious food to keep a person healthy.

# M

**Managed Care Organization (MCO).** An insurance company that the state pays to run a public medical health insurance plan.

**Massive Multimedia Online Role-Playing Games (MMORPGs).** Online role-playing gaming platforms where an unlimited number of people play simultaneously, controlling fictional characters interacting in a fictional world.

**Medical and behavioral assessments.** The process by which health care providers evaluate a patient's physical and mental health.

**Medical (health care) Power of Attorney (POA).** A legal document in which a person gives a family member or trusted friend the right to make health care decisions if the person becomes physical or mentally unable to do so. The form is one of two documents that make up a Durable Power of Attorney (See also Financial Power of Attorney).

**Medically necessary.** Treatments necessary to manage a patient's symptoms.

**Medical specialist.** A provider who is trained and licensed/certified to treat a patient's medical conditions.

**Member's handbook.** A handbook that sums up the benefits that an insurance plan provides. Also available on the company's website, in most cases.

**Mental health (also called behavioral health).** A person's mental well-being, which includes thoughts, feelings, emotions, and behavior.

**Mental Health/Substance Abuse (MHSA) telephone number.** A phone number (listed in the health insurance member's handbook and on the health insurance ID card) that a person must call to get help with questions or problems relating to behavioral health and substance abuse insurance benefits.

**Mental incapacity.** The inability of a person to care for his or her own safety and property because they are mentally unable to make or carry out the necessary decisions.

**Mobile crisis.** A mental health service, usually available through hospitals and community mental health centers, that comes to a person's location to provide an immediate emergency mental health evaluation.

**Mobility supports.** Ways to help people with their physical movements. Examples: wheelchairs, walkers, crutches, canes, etc.

**Mood disorders.** Disorders that affect a person's ability to regulate emotions. Examples: Depression, Bipolar disorder.

# N

**Natural supports.** An informal personal support network consisting of friends, family, neighbors, or others in the community who provide help without being part of a paid service.

**Navigating systems.** The process of finding the right services in agencies and organizations that serve youth and young adults to meet concerns.

**Number codes.** A combination of numbers used by medical and insurance systems to represent patient diagnoses and services provided.

**Nurse Practitioner (NP).** A registered nurse (RN) who has done further advanced training in patient care. An NP can provide many of the same services as a doctor. An NP with special training in psychiatric disorders is called a psychiatric-mental health nurse practitioner (PMHNP).

# O

**Objectives (also known as data points).** In an IEP, specific steps that describe what a youth must learn or accomplish in order to master a stated goal.

**Obligate.** If the school system representative signs an agreement with a youth, the school is legally required to do what the agreement says the school will do for that youth.

**Off-label.** A drug prescribed for a condition or a type of patient it was not originally intended to treat. This means that the United States Food and Drug Administration (FDA) has not yet approved a drug for a certain use in a certain patient group. The doctor may prescribe it anyway, based on his or her own experience and the experience of other doctors and researchers.

**Out-of-network provider.** A provider who is not on the list of a certain insurance company's contracted providers.

**Out-of-pocket.** Costs for services that are not covered by a health insurance policy/plan and that the patient is responsible for paying.

**Over-the-counter medicines.** A medication that can be sold without a prescription from a medical practitioner.

# P

**Parent advocate.** A parent who is involved, aware, and active in the management of his or her youth's care and who speaks up for the youth's best interests.

**Patient portal.** An electronic system used by healthcare providers to maintain records and exchange information with patients and caregivers.

**Pediatric.** Medical field for treating children. Children who see a pediatrician (pediatric doctor) usually switch to another provider at age 18.

**Physical examination records.** The documents in which a person's overall physical health care is described. This record is created after a physical examination.

**Physical or "physical examination."** A medical examination of a person's overall physical (body) health.

**Physician's Assistant (PA).** A person licensed to provide basic care under the supervision of a physician.

**Premium.** The amount a person pays to belong to a health insurance policy/plan. In some plans, this fee is subsidized (paid for, or partly paid for, by a government agency).

**Physician's Assistant (PA).** A person licensed to provide basic care under the supervision of a physician.

**Prescription drug assistance programs.** Programs to help buy medications for people with low income.

**Present level of performance.** A portion of the IEP document that describes a youth's current ability to function and make educational progress in school.

**Primary care provider.** Sometimes known as a family doctor, family practice doctor, or primary care practitioner; a provider who sees patients for general health care needs. A pediatrician or family physician may serve as a child's or youth's primary care provider.

**Primary disorder.** When a person meets the criteria for two different disorders, one disorder will be called the primary (or main) disorder.

**Prior authorization.** See "authorization."

**Private pay insurance plan.** A health insurance plan that the patient pays for himself or he gets through an employer. Young adults can also be part of their parents' insurance plan(s) until age 26.

**Procedures.** Ways of doing things in a certain situation or circumstance.

**Provider.** An individual or organization that provides medical, behavioral health, insurance, or social agency services.

**Psychiatric crisis.** A situation in which a person has a sudden, severe change in behavior that creates a serious risk of harm to that person or someone else.

**Psychiatric medications.** Drugs prescribed by a doctor or nurse practitioner (NP) that treat behavioral health problems.

**Psychiatrist.** A medical doctor (MD) who has done several years of extra training in diseases and disorders of the mind. A psychiatrist can prescribe medications.

# Glossary

**Psychotherapy.** A form of counseling that is commonly known as "talk therapy," but may include other kinds of one-on-one or group treatment.

# R

**Referral.** A primary care provider's order that will allow a patient to see a specialist under the terms of a health insurance plan.

**Regular education program.** A typical educational program designed for youth of a particular age group.

**Reimbursement.** A repayment of money to the patient for money he or she has already spent on services.

**Relationships.** Interactions with people in systems and in the community who can help solve problems and get needed services. (For example, building relationships with case managers, doctors, therapists, and community members who help in navigating systems).

**Release form (also called "Permission to release information").** A form that gives permission for a health, education, insurance, or social services provider to share information with another provider or organization.

**Residential treatment center.** A facility where a patient receives behavioral health or substance abuse treatment 24 hours per day.

**Respite services.** Temporary care for a person with an illness, so regular caregivers, such as parents or other family members, can take breaks.

**Response to Intervention (RTI).** Evidence of methods a school has tried in order to deal with a youth's problem in the regular classroom.

**Right to privacy.** A patient's right, under certain conditions, to keep personal information private and not share with others.

**Role-Playing Games (RPGs).** A type of video game where the gamer controls a fictional character who interacts with other characters in an imaginary world.

**Roles.** The different jobs people and providers perform in certain situations. For example, it is a patient's role to describe symptoms they are experiencing, whereas it is the doctor's role to diagnose the condition.

**Rule-out.** A condition that would disqualify a youth from being certified as having a disability under IDEA 2004. For example, if the main reason for a youth's lack of progress is poor attendance at school, a behavioral health issue alone would not be enough to qualify that youth to receive special educational services.

# S

**Scams.** Illegal attempts to trick others into giving money, usually done by telephone or online.

**School evaluation (also called a "comprehensive assessment").** An evaluation performed by the school system; this evaluation examines many areas of a youth's behavior, abilities, and school performance.

**Secondary disorder (also called a comorbid diagnosis).** A term used in medical and behavioral health systems to mean a person meets the criteria for more than one disorder.

**Service coordinator.** If a youth is eligible for services because of a medical, behavioral, or developmental problem, a person called a service coordinator may be assigned to help the family create a plan for getting treatment and other services.

**Sexual dysfunction.** Difficulty or inability to perform or enjoy sexual activities that are typical for a person.

**Sexuality.** A person's sexual feelings or preferences.

**Sliding scale.** A system in which people are charged fees according to what they can afford to pay.

**Special education.** Services and methods used to educate students with disabilities who qualify under the federal IDEA 2004 law.

**Specialized crisis services.** A unit of trained staff that comes to a youth's location to assess his or her need for emergency care.

**Standardized assessment tools.** Tests commonly used to evaluate behavioral health or educational problems. Some typical standard assessment tools include cognitive and adaptive tests, psychological evaluations, developmental evaluations, and educational evaluations.

**State child protection agency.** A government agency responsible for evaluating and protecting the physical, emotional, and mental well-being of children and youth.

**Subsidized.** Paid for by an organization or government agency.

**Supplemental Security Income (SSI).** A monthly government payment available to (a) low-income families with children under age 18 who have disabilities and (b) low-income adults with disabilities.

**Symptoms.** Signs of disease that may include physical changes, thoughts, feelings, and behaviors.

**System of care.** An agreement between different agencies in a community to collaborate (cooperate) in providing different types of services to a certain population. Some communities have "systems of care" that provide a range of services and supports for youth with mental health problems. These services and supports might include therapy, help with housing and food issues, peer support, and connections to education or training programs.

**System representative.** See "LEA representative."

**Systems.** Organizations and agencies that provide treatment or services (for example, mental health systems).

**Telemedicine.** Medical or behavioral health assistance provided through the Internet or videoconferencing software.

**Therapeutic dose.** The amount of a medication that is effective to treat the patient's symptoms.

**Therapist.** A person licensed by the state to give treatment for physical health, behavioral health, and/or developmental disorders.

**Timeline.** The time frame in which a person or organization must respond to an action taken by another person or organization. (For example, if a person files a complaint, the agency involved must respond within a certain number of days. This period is called the timeline.)

**Titrate or Titration.** The process of increasing a person's medication dosage from a small amount of a drug to a larger dose over a period of days or weeks.

**Transition.** A term used in education law to mean a period of years between the late teens and early twenties, when a young person's task is to gain the skills needed for independent living.

**Transition plan.** A set of goals for a student's transition after completing high school. By law, the transition plan must be included in the student's Individualized Education Program (IEP) beginning at age 16.

**Transition to adulthood (also called emerging adulthood).** The period between age 14 to 26 (up to age 30 in the opinion of some), in which a person is in the process of becoming an adult.

**Transportation supports.** Help with getting to places for education, work, and community life. Transportation supports might include a disability discount for bus transportation, a special education bus, or a program that reimburses (pays back) for a transportation expense.

**Trauma.** A serious, negative event in a person's life that can affect behavior, emotions, and physical health. Examples: sexual abuse, family violence, death of a close relative, or involvement in a natural disaster.

**Treatment plan.** A medical plan that lists treatment steps, which can help a youth or young adult reach goals created with help from providers and others.

**Unstable housing.** A place for a youth to live or stay now, but the youth may have to leave soon (due to safety concerns, can't pay rent, etc.).

**Utilization review, utilization reviewer.** The process by which insurance companies decide whether certain health services are covered by a person's health insurance plan. The company employs the reviewers, who are often nurses or social workers.

**V**

**Vocational rehabilitation.** A state government agency that helps people with disabilities find jobs and gain skills to succeed in the workforce.

# Medication Abbreviations

Here are some abbreviations you might find on prescription forms, on orders for lab tests, and in your medical files:

| | |
|---|---|
| b.i.d. | give medication twice a day |
| CBC | complete blood count |
| ECG | electrocardiogram (looks for heart problems) |
| EEG | electro-encephalogram (looks for brain problems) |
| g | gram (unit of measurement) |
| h.s. | at bedtime |
| kg | kilogram |
| L | liter |
| mg | milligram |
| NSAID | Non-steroidal anti-inflammatory drug (such as aspirin) |
| O2 | oxygen |
| OTC | over-the-counter (non-prescription) |
| P.O. | by mouth |
| P.R. | rectally (in your bottom) |
| p.r.n. | as needed |
| q.i.d. | every day |
| quid. | four times a day |
| RBC | red blood-cell count |
| S.L. | sublingual (under the tongue) |
| t.i.d. | three times a day |
| WBC | white blood-cell count |

*Source: Linda Zweifel, Former Director of Programs, NAMI Montgomery County, Texas. Used with author's permission.*

CPSIA information can be obtained
at www.ICGtesting.com
Printed in the USA
LVHW072047281220
675127LV00003B/70